Routine

A Practical Guide to Taking Control of Your Day

(How to Create the Ultimate Daily Routine for More Energy and Success)

Ryan Judson

Published By **Chris David**

Ryan Judson

All Rights Reserved

Routine: A Practical Guide to Taking Control of Your Day (How to Create the Ultimate Daily Routine for More Energy and Success)

ISBN 978-1-7752619-4-0

No part of this guidebook shall be reproduced in any form without permission in writing from the publisher except in the case of brief quotations embodied in critical articles or reviews.

Legal & Disclaimer

The information contained in this book is not designed to replace or take the place of any form of medicine or professional medical advice. The information in this book has been provided for educational & entertainment purposes only.

The information contained in this book has been compiled from sources deemed reliable, and it is accurate to the best of the Author's knowledge; however, the Author cannot guarantee its accuracy and validity and cannot be held liable for any errors or omissions. Changes are periodically made to this book. You must consult your doctor or get professional medical advice before using any of the suggested remedies, techniques, or information in this book.

Table Of Contents

Chapter 1: Get Enough Sleep 1

Chapter 2: Wake Up Early 6

Chapter 3: Hydrate And Nourish Your Body
.... 13

Chapter 4: Exercise And Stretch 19

Chapter 5: Practice Mindfulness 25

Chapter 6: Plan Your Day 29

Chapter 7: Get Ready For The Day 35

Chapter 8: Adjusting Your Morning
Routine For Different Seasons 41

Chapter 9: The Benefits Of Journaling In
The Morning 45

Chapter 10: Incorporating Self-Care Into
Your Morning Routine 53

Chapter 11: Creating A Family-Friendly
Morning Routine 59

Chapter 12: Troubleshooting Your Morning
Routine 63

Chapter 13: Tracking Your Progress And Staying Accountable 69

Chapter 14: The Science Of Habits 74

Chapter 15: Identifying Your Goals 80

Chapter 16: Designing Effective Habits .. 86

Chapter 17: Creating A Balanced Routine 93

Chapter 18: Overcoming Challenges And Staying Consistent 100

Chapter 19: Nurturing Physical And Mental Well-Being 107

Chapter 20: Cultivating Meaningful Relationships 114

Chapter 21: Embracing Lifelong Learning And Growth 121

Chapter 22: Embracing Mindfulness And Finding Inner Peace............................. 127

Chapter 23: Understanding Routine And Happiness 135

Chapter 24: Crafting Your Happiness Boosting Routine 144

Chapter 25: Productivity And Time Management Routine 149

Chapter 26: Routine For Physical Well-Being... 152

Chapter 27: Winding Down For Peaceful Sleep.. 159

Chapter 28: Maintaining Consistency... 167

Chapter 29: Find The Right Time 176

Chapter 30: Choosing The Appropriate Space 179

Chapter 1: Get Enough Sleep

A success morning habitual is built on getting sufficient sleep. Sleep is essential for our physical, highbrow, and emotional fitness, and it devices the tone for a way we enjoy and characteristic during the day. Without accurate sufficient sleep, we also can experience tired, irritable, and unproductive, that might have a horrific effect on our stylish top notch of lifestyles.

Adults should strive for 7-nine hours of sleep every night time time time. Many dad and mom, however, struggle to accumulate this requirement because of worrying schedules, pressure, and precise instances that might disrupt our sleep.

Here are a few recommendations for buying sufficient sleep and incorporating it into your morning recurring:

Create a constant sleep schedule:

Try going to mattress and waking up at the same time each day, even on weekends. This helps to alter your frame's inner clock and makes falling asleep and waking up much less complex.

Create a snooze-inducing environment:

To encourage a restful sleep environment, make your mattress room darkish, quiet, and cold. To prevent distractions, use blackout curtains, earplugs, or a white noise device.

Limit show display time earlier than bedtime:

The blue slight emitted thru virtual gadgets can interrupt our herbal sleep-wake cycle, making it hard to go to sleep. Limit your show time before bedtime, or use blue moderate-blocking off eyewear or device settings.

Avoid caffeine and alcohol:

Caffeine and alcohol can intervene with our sleep and make it tough to fall and stay asleep. Avoid or restriction your consumption of those materials earlier than going to mattress.

Practice relaxation strategies:

Engage in soothing sports activities in advance than bedtime, collectively with studying, having a warmness bathtub, or going for walks closer to yoga or meditation. These can help to loosen up your mind and inspire a awesome night time time time's sleep.

Invest in a comfortable slumbering floor and pillows:

A cushty snoozing surroundings can decorate the exquisite of your sleep extensively. Invest in a outstanding bed and pillows at the manner to provide your frame with enough assist and luxury.

Seek professional help if crucial:

If you have got got persistent sleep troubles or insomnia, seek advice from a healthcare practitioner. They can test your sound asleep behavior and endorse treatment selections alongside aspect remedy or counseling.

Use a sleep-monitoring app:

If you're having problems tracking your sleep, recollect using sleep-tracking software or an software application that tracks your sleep styles and gives recommendations on a manner to decorate your sleep terrific. Some apps even combine with smart system, along with smart mattresses and pillows, to offer individualized sleep hints.

Address any underlying sleep problems:

If you experience signs and symptoms like snoring, breathing pauses, or immoderate daylight hours sleepiness, you could have an underlying sleep scenario like sleep apnea. Consult a medical medical health practitioner about present procedure a nap take a look at to diagnose and address any underlying sleep troubles.

Avoid taking too many naps in the route of the day:

While a quick nap in the course of the day will let you revel in greater energized, taking too many naps can intrude together with your capacity to fall and live asleep at night. If you need to nap at some point of the day, keep it short (about 20-1/2-hour) and early within the afternoon.

Remember that getting sufficient sleep is ready more than truely the quantity of hours you spend in bed; it's also approximately the first-rate of your sleep. To increase the exceptional of your sleep, cause to create a peaceful and comfortable drowsing surroundings and continuously follow wholesome sleep hygiene schedules. With steady try, you could establish healthy sleep habits that assist a a achievement morning habitual and regular properly-being.

Chapter 2: Wake Up Early

Waking up early is a effective addiction that has the capability to decorate your life. Early risers are greater green, have better mental readability, and feel greater power all day. While waking early can look like a hard mission, with steady attempt, it may grow to be a natural and exciting detail of your morning habitual. Work with the ones pointers if you really need to wake up early and make it a dependancy:

Establish a normal sleep time table:

As stated within the previous financial disaster, retaining a normal sleep time table is important for obtaining enough sleep and waking up early. Set a everyday bedtime and wake-up time as a way to can help you advantage 7-9 hours of sleep every night time time time, and try to keep on with it as lots as feasible.

Use an alarm clock:

Use an alarm clock to make sure which you awaken at the same time each day. To assist ease you into wakefulness, use an alarm sound this is slight and first-class in preference to harsh or loud.

Put your alarm clock across the room, far from your mattress:

Set your alarm clock across the room, an extended way out of your bed so that you should break out from bed to reveal it off. This prevents you from hitting the snooze button and encourages you to start your day.

Avoid dozing:

As tempting as using the snooze button may additionally additionally additionally appear, it is able to make you enjoy more fatigued and gradual. Instead, break out from bed as quick as your alarm is going off and begin your morning routine.

Drink water:

A glass of water first element inside the morning can help hydrate your frame and kickstart your metabolism. It can also make you sense extra extensive awake and aware.

Get moving:

Do some modest bodily interest, which include stretching or going for a quick walk, to get your blood flowing and your frame awake. This can help to enhance your temper and strength ranges.

Have a motive to break out from mattress:

Having a cause and purpose to get off the bed can assist encourage you to get away from bed. Having a cause to rouse, whether or no longer or now not it's far for a morning exercising, meditation exercise, or genuinely having breakfast at the side of your circle of relatives, will permit you to get began.

Create a morning ordinary:

Developing a regular morning routine can help in making waking up early a addiction.

Start with simple conduct like making your bed, brushing your tooth, or operating toward gratitude, and step by step upload greater sports activities activities as you get used to getting up early.

Get herbal slight:

Natural light exposure can help modify your frame's natural sleep-wake cycle and make it simpler to awaken in the morning. Allow herbal mild in by manner of beginning your blinds or curtains, or try making an funding in a mild treatment lamp to copy herbal moderate.

Be patient and chronic:

Waking up early does now not arise in a unmarried day. Establishing a consistent early morning addiction takes time, staying power, and endurance. If you are making a mistake or bypass over an afternoon, do no longer be too hard on your self. Instead, offer hobby for your accomplishments and maintain running in the direction of your purpose of waking up early.

Avoid the use of electronics earlier than mattress:

Using devices, like cellular phones and tablets, in advance than bed can disrupt your body's natural sleep-wake cycle, making it extra hard to fall asleep. To promote better sleep and make it less complicated to wake up inside the morning, keep away from the use of devices for at least an hour earlier than bedtime.

Establish a calming bedtime habitual:

A relaxing middle of the night ordinary can help join up your body that it is time to sleep, making it plenty less complex to go to sleep. Activities which includes taking a warm bathtub, analyzing a ebook, or practising relaxation strategies like deep respiration or meditation.

Maintain a chilly and dark surroundings on your bedroom:

A cool and darkish environment can help sell better sleep and make it a whole lot much less complex to wake up in the morning. Adopt a snug mattress room temperature (approximately 60-sixty seven stages Fahrenheit) and use blackout curtains or a snooze masks to block out any mild which could intrude together along with your sleep.

Avoid caffeine and alcohol in advance than mattress:

Caffeine and alcohol earlier than bed can disrupt your sleep and make it tough to evoke in the morning. To make sure better sleep, keep away from those materials at least four-6 hours earlier than bedtime.

Consistency on weekends:

While it is able to be tempting to sleep in on weekends, adjusting your sleep agenda have to make waking up early during the week more tough. Try to have a ordinary sleep and wake-up time even on weekends, to help increase a regular sleep time table.

By incorporating those tips into your day by day regular, you can set up a everyday addiction of waking up early and reaping the advantages of a powerful and energizing morning normal. Remember that waking up early is ready greater than in fact the time at the clock; it's also approximately the mind-set and conduct that include it. With persistence, persistence, and self-control, you could awaken feeling refreshed, energized, and prepared to address the day beforehand.

Chapter 3: Hydrate And Nourish Your Body

The morning is the right time for placing the mood for the the relaxation of your day. One of the great techniques to carry out this is to begin your day with sufficient hydration and nourishment. After all, your body has been fasting for severa hours at the identical time as you slept, and it's miles critical to provide it with the nutrients it calls for to perform optimally.

This bankruptcy will discover the advantages of hydration and nourishment, similarly to a manner to put in force those practices into your morning habitual.

Why Hydration is Important

Hydration is critical for a wholesome existence. Your frame is made from about 60% water, and each device in your frame is based upon on it to function nicely.

Increases Energy Levels:

Dehydration reasons your body to art work harder to feature effectively. This can bring about feelings of exhaustion and sluggishness. Drinking water inside the morning permit you to enjoy greater alert and energized.

Aids digestion:

Water is crucial for correct digestion. It permits inside the digestion of food, the absorption of nutrients, and the removal of waste. Drinking water first issue in the morning can help kickstart your digestion and encourage regularity.

Help in Weight Loss:

Drinking water should make you enjoy fuller, which can lessen your urge for food and prevent overeating. It can also help to beautify your metabolism, which permits you to burn extra strength at some stage in the day.

Improves Skin Health:

Dehydration can result in dry, silly pores and skin. Water can assist hydrate your pores and skin from inner, giving it a wholesome, radiant appearance.

How to Stay Hydrated inside the Morning

Now that we have were given had been given mentioned the benefits of hydration, let's communicate approximately a manner to consist of it into your morning routine.

Drink a Glass of Water First Thing within the Morning:

When you wake up, the primary detail you want to do is drink a glass of water. This can help in rehydrating your frame after an prolonged night time time's sleep.

Keep a Water Bottle close by:

Keep a water bottle to your bedside or in your relaxation room so that you can drink water as soon as you wake up.

Infuse Your Water:

If plain water bores you, try infusing it with fruit or herbs for taste. Lemon, cucumber, mint, and ginger are all delicious flavors.

Set a hydration intention:

Try to consume a specific quantity of water in advance than midday. This can assist make sure which you drink enough water within the direction of the day.

Why Nourishment is Important

Nutrition, further to hydration, is vital for max fitness. To feature effectively, your frame desires a nicely-balanced combination of vitamins.

Here are a number of the benefits of nourishing your body first difficulty in the morning:

Energy:

Eating a properly-balanced breakfast will help your body get the strength it desires to start the day. This will allow you to live alert and focused eventually of the day.

Promotes Weight Management:

Eating breakfast can help to lessen cravings and prevent overeating later in the day. It can assist to enhance your metabolism, permitting you to burn more electricity at a few degree inside the day.

Improves Brain Function:

In order to function well, your thoughts desires glucose (a shape of sugar). Breakfast can help your mind get the glucose it desires to assume properly and recognition.

Improves Mood:

Eating a nutritious breakfast will help to normalize your blood sugar degrees, that can enhance your temper and reduce signs of hysteria or sadness.

Tips for Nourishing Your Body within the Morning

Here are some pointers for nourishing your body inside the morning and incorporating it into your morning ordinary:

Eat a Well-Balanced Breakfast:

Aim for a breakfast that includes protein, wholesome fat, and complex carbohydrates. This can embody such things as eggs, avocado, entire-grain toast, or a protein-packed smoothie.

Plan earlier of time:

If you're pressed for time in the morning, prepare your breakfast the night time before. This should include in a unmarried day oats, pre-made smoothie packs, or difficult-boiled eggs.

Avoid Sugary Foods:

While a sugary pastry or cereal can seem appealing, those food can reason a drop in energy levels later inside the morning. Instead, select out meals robust in fiber and protein.

Chapter 4: Exercise And Stretch

While many people companion exercise and stretching with overdue afternoon or middle of the night exercise physical games or sports, incorporating those strategies into your morning everyday can provide numerous benefits. By exercise and stretching within the morning, you may decorate your power tiers, beautify your temper, and set your self up for a effective and focused day.

In this financial wreck, we're going to find out the advantages of morning exercising and stretching, the way to include them into your everyday, and what forms of sports activities and stretches to try.

Benefits of Exercise and Stretching inside the Morning

Boost Energy Levels:

Exercise reasons the discharge of endorphins, which could make you enjoy more energized and alert. Starting your day with exercising can provide you with a natural power enhance to help you get via the morning.

Improve Mood:

Exercise is a natural mood enhancer. Exercise will can help you sense more positive and happy inside the morning through the release of endorphins and reducing pressure chemical compounds.

Increase Productivity:

Studies have indicated that exercising improves cognitive competencies, which incorporates concentration, memory, and creativity. You can enhance your productivity and attention within the direction of the day with the aid of workout in the morning.

Reduce Stress:

Starting your day with exercising assist you to reduce stress, that could have numerous nice affects in your bodily and intellectual fitness.

How to Include Exercise and Stretching in Your Morning Routine

Start small:

If you're no longer used to workout in the morning, set small dreams for your self. Even 15-20 minutes of workout or stretching can enhance your electricity tiers and attitude.

Plan beforehand of time:

Lay out your exercise garments and device the night time time before to make it clean to begin within the morning. You also can set up your health program or look at a exercising video or app.

Find a Workout Partner:

A exercise pal or companion will will will let you live stimulated and responsible. Consider enlisting the assist of a gymnasium companion that will help you together with your early time table.

Mix it up:

Don't feel obligated to have a take a look at the identical workout software every morning. To hold subjects glowing, blend it up with one-of-a-type varieties of exercise or try new exercise routines.

Types of Exercises and Stretches to Try

Yoga:

Yoga is an exceptional method to stretch and improve your muscle tissues at the same time as concurrently amusing your mind. You can try a yoga video or app, or you may in fact practice a few important yoga poses.

Cardio:

If you need to get your coronary coronary heart price up inside the morning, attempt a few aerobic exercise workouts which include jumping jacks, excessive knees, or taking walks in region.

Strength Training:

Strength education is an tremendous way to boom muscle and beautify famous health. For a quick morning workout, attempt the use of loose weights or resistance bands.

Stretching:

Stretching assist you to increase your flexibility and relieve muscle strain. Try a few easy stretches, like hamstring stretches, quad stretches, and shoulder rolls.

Pilates:

Pilates is a low-effect form of exercising that focuses on middle energy and posture development. Consider which incorporates some Pilates bodily video games, much like the hundred, plank, or roll-up, into your morning habitual.

HIIT:

High-depth interval training (HIIT) is a type of exercise that consists of brief bursts of intensive activity accompanied with the aid of rest durations. HIIT exercising workouts are frequently short and powerful, making them an brilliant preference for busy mornings.

Walking or Jogging:

Walking or on foot inside the morning may be an remarkable way to get some fresh air, smooth your thoughts, and get your blood flowing.

Dance:

Dancing is an brilliant manner to get your coronary heart price up and your temper up. Consider searching a dance video or being attentive to a dance aggregate to enhance your morning ordinary.

Remember to pay interest for your body and select out physical games that be simply proper for you. If you're new to fitness or have any fitness issues, speak with a scientific medical doctor earlier than beginning any new exercise plan.

Chapter 5: Practice Mindfulness

The exercising of being absolutely gift inside the moment, without judgment or distraction, is called mindfulness. Adopting mindfulness into your morning ordinary let you begin your day with a easy and calm mind.

Here are a few morning mindfulness practices to try:

Meditation:

Meditation is an notable approach to cultivating mindfulness. Spend a few minutes each morning sitting quietly and focusing to your respiration. If you are new to meditation, there are many apps and guided meditations to get you commenced.

Mindful breathing:

You can exercise mindfulness even in case you do not have time for an entire meditation session by the usage of manner of focusing to your breath. Take a few deep breaths and consciousness on the movement of air internal and from your body.

Gratitude workout:

Practicing gratitude will will let you expand a more high-quality mind-set about lifestyles. Spend some moments each morning reflecting on some thing you are thankful for. It can be as easy as a heat blanket or a cup of coffee.

Body experiment:

A frame take a look at is a mindfulness approach in which you awareness on every part of your body in flip. Each morning, spend a couple of minutes scanning your body from head to toe, noting any areas of tension or soreness.

Mindful movement:

Mindful moves, together with yoga or tai chi, will will let you cultivate mindfulness even as moreover exercising your frame. Consider together with moderate stretches or yoga positions on your morning habitual.

Mindfulness will allow you to begin your day with a clean and calm mind, however it could additionally have numerous other advantages, which includes:

Stress and anxiety reduce fee

Improving Concentration and Focus

Enhancing self-popularity

Improving emotional law

You'll be putting yourself up for a more green and exciting day in case you exercise mindfulness within the morning. So, strive mindfulness for a couple of minutes every morning and be conscious how it is able to enhance your mornings and your lifestyles.

Mindful Eating:

Mindful Eating consists of taking note of the food you're ingesting further to the manner it makes you sense. Take some time with breakfast, savoring the taste, texture, and aroma of every meal. This will let you feel glad and similarly energized at some degree within the day.

Mindful Journaling:

Writing in a mag let you easy your thoughts and sell focus. Spend a couple of minutes each morning writing down your thoughts, feelings, and intentions for the day. This assist you to live focused and stimulated for the duration of the day.

Mindful Listening:

Each morning, take a few seconds to pay attention to the sounds round you, whether or not or now not or now not they be birds chirping outdoor or the sound of your coffee brewing. You'll revel in more grounded and targeted if you recognition on the present 2d.

Mindful Visualization:

Mindful Visualization consists of the usage of your imagination to generate a mental photo of a favored very last consequences. Spend some moments every morning visualizing yourself reaching your goals for the day. This helps to keep you endorsed and targeted on your dreams.

Remember that operating closer to mindfulness is a talent that goals time and persistence. Begin with a few minutes of mindfulness meditation each morning and steadily work your way as a lot as longer periods of mindfulness workout. You'll be setting yourself up for a extra peaceful efficient, and pleasurable day in case you undertake mindfulness into your morning exercise.

Chapter 6: Plan Your Day

Planning your day is an powerful element of a a success morning ordinary. By taking a couple of minutes every morning to devise out your day, you may boom your productivity, reduce strain and anxiety, and make the maximum of it gradual.

Here are a few hints for making plans your day:

Make a to-do list:

Start via manner of making a listing of the duties you want to carry out for the day. This will let you in very last targeted and on direction in a few unspecified time in the future of the day. Prioritize your chores constant with their significance and urgency.

Schedule your day:

Once you have got your to-do list, it's time to time table your day. Block off time for every task in your list, ensuring to transport away a few buffer time in case topics take longer than anticipated. Be positive to schedule breaks eventually of the day to offer your thoughts and body a threat to relaxation and recharge.

Use a planner or calendar:

Using a planner or calendar can be a great way to hold music of your time table and stay prepared. Choose a planner or calendar that works for you, whether or not or no longer it's far a paper planner or an app for your telephone.

Be sensible:

When making plans your day, it's vital to be practical about what you may accomplish. Don't try to cram too many duties into some time desk, or you can become feeling beaten and stressed. Be honest with yourself about how an awful lot you can genuinely get done in an afternoon.

Adjust your plan as preferred:

Things do not generally bypass as planned, and this is k. Be organized to alter your plan as needed in the path of the day. If a few element sudden comes up, be flexible and alter your time table as a result.

By taking the time to devise your day, you may be capable of method your obligations with greater attention and clarity. You'll furthermore be tons a great deal much less in all likelihood to revel in overwhelmed or compelled, because of the truth you can have a clean plan for what you want to carry out.

Here are a few more benefits of planning your day:

Increased productivity:

By planning your day, you'll be able to use a while greater successfully, that may growth your productiveness.

Reduced stress and anxiety:

When you have were given a clear plan for the day, you may revel in greater on top of things and much less stressful.

Better time manage:

Planning your day assist you to make the most of a while and keep away from losing time on unimportant duties.

Greater feel of accomplishment:

When you're able to test off duties out of your to-do listing inside the direction of the day, you'll sense a feel of success and pride.

Reflect on the day before today:

In addition to making plans for the modern day, it is able to be useful to reflect on the day past. Take a few minutes each morning to take a look at what you done and what you failed to get to. This assist you to make adjustments to your time desk and end up aware about any patterns or conduct that may be preserving you returned.

Set desires for the day:

Setting desires for the day will assist you to live inspired and centered. Consider what you want to do for the day and make specific, measurable goals. This will let you in staying on track and keep away from distractions from a lot much less important chores.

Use generation for your advantage:

There are many apps and tools available that can help you plan your day and stay organized. From virtual calendars to task manage apps, find out the gear that paintings brilliant for you and include them into your morning everyday.

Involve others:

If you have got a group or colleagues which you art work with, contain them in your making plans system. Schedule conferences or take a look at-ins within the path of the day to keep all of us at the equal net page and ensure that everybody is walking toward the identical goals.

Be flexible:

While planning your day is crucial, it is also crucial to be flexible. Life is unpredictable, and things do now not generally pass as deliberate. Be prepared to alter your time table as wished and do not get too caught up in sticking to a rigid plan.

Chapter 7: Get Ready For The Day

Getting equipped for the day is an important part of any morning recurring. It not most effective lets in you appearance and experience your amazing, but it could furthermore set the tone on your day and decorate yourself belief.

Here are a few suggestions that will help you get prepared for the day in the maximum efficient and effective way viable:

Wash your face:

The first step in getting organized for the day is to scrub your face. To get rid of any dirt or oil that has accrued in a single day, use a mild cleaner. This will assist your pores and skin feel easy and refreshed and can also help prevent breakouts.

Moisturize:

Use a moisturizer after washing your face to preserve your pores and pores and skin hydrated and keep away from dryness. This is specifically critical within the route of the wintry weather months even as the air is dry and might purpose your pores and skin to revel in tight and uncomfortable.

Brush your enamel:

Brushing your enamel is an crucial a part of your morning ordinary. Not simplest does it help hold your enamel and gums healthful, but it is able to furthermore freshen your breath and beautify your self belief.

Take a tub:

Taking a shower will can help you wake up and experience refreshed. Use a body wash or cleaning soap to smooth your pores and skin, and take into account the use of a scrub to exfoliate any lifeless pores and pores and skin cells. This can leave your pores and pores and pores and skin silky and easy.

Get dressed:

Choosing what to put on for the day can be a a laugh and innovative part of your morning everyday. Choose clothes that make you sense comfortable and confident, and remember laying them out the night time in advance than to keep time in the morning.

Style your hair:

Whether you have got were given were given prolonged or brief hair, styling your hair permit you to revel in put together and geared up to take on the day. Choose a fashion that works for your hair kind and the event, and recollect the use of hair merchandise like mousse or hairspray to hold your style in area.

Apply makeup (if desired):

If you positioned on make-up, this is the time to apply it. Start with a smooth face and look at a primer to help your make-up go on easily. Then, exercise basis, concealer, and a few distinct face products you operate. Finish with eye make-up and lip merchandise, and recollect to combo properly to keep away from harsh lines.

Organize your belongings:

Before you leave the house, take a few minutes to set up your own home. Make positive you have got the whole thing you need for the day, including your cellular cellphone, wallet, keys, and every different essentials. This let you keep away from the stress of looking for out of place objects later inside the day.

Take a 2d to middle yourself:

Finally, in advance than you head out the door, take a 2d to middle yourself. Take a deep breath, set an purpose for the day, and visualize your self challenge your desires. This will will let you begin the day with a tremendous and targeted mindset.

Pack your bag:

If you have were given a busy day earlier, ensure you % your bag with all the devices you need for the day. This can encompass paintings substances, snacks, water bottles, and each other requirements. By making prepared everything earlier, you can shop time and keep away from the strain of scrambling to discover items later within the day.

Check the weather:

Before choosing what to place on for the day, check the weather forecast. This will let you get dressed correctly and keep away from getting stuck inside the rain or snow without right clothing. Knowing the weather can also assist you plan your day because of this, which includes bringing an umbrella or selecting indoor sports.

Practice accurate hygiene:

While showering and combing your teeth are critical elements of having ready for the day, operating towards right hygiene at some point of the day is equally important. This can encompass washing your fingers often, the use of hand sanitizer, and carrying tissues or handkerchiefs to keep away from spreading germs.

Adopt self-care:

Getting prepared for the day may be a top notch opportunity to include a few self-care practices into your recurring. This can embody utilising a face masks or moisturizer, using a scented lotion, or taking a couple of minutes to stretch or meditate. By prioritizing self-care in the morning, you may set a powerful tone for the relaxation of the day.

Don't rush:

Rushing through your morning normal can depart you feeling harassed and worrying for the rest of the day. Try to present yourself lots of time inside the morning to get prepared without feeling rushed. This can also recommend waking up earlier or simplifying your ordinary to preserve time.

Chapter 8: Adjusting Your Morning Routine For Different Seasons

As the seasons change, so need to your morning routine. Different temperatures, climate styles, and daytime can all have an effect on the way you revel in inside the morning and what sports you prioritize.

By adjusting your morning ordinary for wonderful seasons, you may optimize your health and properly-being all yr round.

Winter:

In the wintry climate months, it could be in particular difficult to break out from bed in the morning because of colder temperatures and shorter daytime. To triumph over this, maintain in mind adjusting your everyday to include greater time for rest and self-care. This can embody taking a warmth bath or shower, practicing yoga or meditation, or indulging in a heat cup of tea or coffee. Additionally, ensure to dress because it want to be for the weather and offer yourself greater time to tour in case of snow or ice.

Spring:

Spring is a time of renewal and increase, and your morning habitual can reflect this. Take benefit of the longer daylight via adopting greater outside sports, which includes going for a morning walk or run. Additionally, recollect incorporating more clean fruits and veggies into your breakfast to take benefit of the seasonal produce. Finally, make sure to preserve an eye fixed fixed on any seasonal allergic reactions and take suitable measures, which includes taking hypersensitive reaction treatment or keeping off outdoor sports sports ultimately of pinnacle pollen hours.

Summer:

The hotter weather and longer sunlight hours may be encouraging at a few diploma in the summer season months. Take gain of this by means of incorporating greater outdoor sports into your morning ordinary, together with swimming or hiking. Additionally, make certain to shield your pores and pores and skin from the solar's volatile rays by means of way of the use of sunscreen and wearing a hat. Finally, stay hydrated thru ingesting loads of water throughout the day, mainly at some point of out of doors sports sports.

Fall:

As the weather starts to settle down and the times get shorter, it is crucial to adjust your regular because of this. Consider including greater warmness hearty components to your breakfast, along side oatmeal or eggs. Additionally, make certain to get wearing layers to stay cushty as temperatures variety in the direction of the day. Finally, take advantage of the converting foliage through incorporating a nature stroll or hike into your morning regular.

Year-round modifications:

While each season has its specific demanding situations and possibilities, there are a few adjustments you may make for your morning recurring that are beneficial all year round. For instance, make certain to prioritize getting enough sleep and staying hydrated, irrespective of the season. Additionally, consider incorporating mindfulness or relaxation techniques, which include meditation or deep breathing, into your everyday to help lessen pressure and tension.

By adjusting your morning ordinary for one-of-a-kind seasons, you could optimize your physical and intellectual health all 365 days round. By being conscious of the converting weather patterns and daytime, you could create a ordinary that allows your everyday well-being and permits you begin every time without work on the right foot.

Chapter 9: The Benefits Of Journaling In The Morning

Journaling is a superb workout to enhance your mental health and regular well-being. It can set up a powerful tone for the day in advance and help you navigate any issues that would rise up if finished in the morning.

In this chapter, we are going to have a have a look at the blessings of morning journaling and provide some tips on how to get started out.

Helps you're making clean your thoughts and emotions:

Writing down your ideas and emotions will let you make sense of them and easy any confusion or ambiguity. When you take some time to install writing down your thoughts, you can have a higher information of what goes on in your head and may be capable of art work through any uncomfortable feelings or studies.

Promotes self-reflected picture and self-recognition:

Journaling encourages self-reflection and self-interest via allowing you to reflect to your existence and tales, that could result in multiplied awareness and private growth. When you have a look at your thoughts and behaviors, you may be able to apprehend patterns and make proper modifications if you want to decorate your first-rate of life.

Reduces pressure and anxiety:

Journaling is a fantastic strain reliever and could allow you to in dealing with tension and fear. You can relieve any pent-up stress or tension thru writing out your thoughts and emotions, making you revel in extra cushty and snug.

Enhances creativity and problem-solving abilities:

Journaling in the morning can extensively improve your creativity and problem-solving competencies. When you write down your thoughts and thoughts, you could skip deeper into them and give you easy answers to troubles.

Increases gratitude and boosts temper:

Writing down stuff you're grateful for inside the morning assist you to start your day on a first-rate take a look at and beautify your mental u.S.A.. You can exchange your mind-set and enjoy more pleased and fulfilled thru focusing on the excessive nice elements of your life.

Increases self-recognition:

Journaling in the morning lets you mirror on your mind, emotions, and behaviors, allowing you to get a better statistics of your self. This can lead to advanced self-attention, it surely is important for personal improvement and boom.

Enhances creativity:

By giving yourself the freedom to put in writing without judgment or expectation, you could tap into your creativity and provide you with new thoughts or answers to troubles.

Boosts productivity:

Journaling in the morning will let you prioritize your goals and duties for the day, which can boom productivity and typical performance.

Promotes gratitude:

By reflecting on what you're thankful for in existence, you can create an excellent thoughts-set and enhance your common properly-being.

Improves highbrow readability:

Writing down your mind will can help you set up your thoughts and make clear your questioning, resulting in stepped forward intellectual clarity and popularity.

Provides a feel of achievement:

Completion of your morning every day journaling exercising can provide you with a sense of fulfillment and set up a exceptional tone for the the rest of the day.

Overall, adopting a morning journaling exercising into your normal will let you in beginning your day with a smooth thoughts, increase your creativity and productivity, and beautify your intellectual fitness and properly-being.

Getting Started with Morning Journaling

Find a peaceful and comfortable vicinity to write:

Find an area wherein you could concentrate with out distractions and wherein you could experience cushty and calm.

Set apart time each morning to mag:

Even if it's miles only some minutes, set apart time every morning to mag.

Allow your self to write down freely and without judgment:

Allow yourself to install writing freely and without judgment. Allow your thoughts to go together with the float onto the net page without annoying approximately grammar or spelling.

Experiment with super turns on:

Try exploring particular pocket book topics, including writing about your day's desires or reflecting on a preceding experience. This can help preserve your writing exciting and new.

Use a gratitude mag:

Include a gratitude mag for your morning recurring with the aid of way of jotting down stuff you're thankful for. This can useful resource inside the improvement of a more wonderful mindset and the enhancement of sentiments of happiness and contentment.

Use a mag in that you experience writing:

Choose a magazine in which you are extremely blissful to write down. Find a few thing you need using and that motivates you to install writing, whether or no longer it's miles a exquisite pocket book or virtual journaling software.

Experiment with unique writing devices:

To add a few originality and variant for your writing, bear in mind the usage of unique writing gear, collectively with coloured pens or markers. This may want to make the technique extra fun and thrilling.

Start small:

If you're new to journaling, start with only some mins each morning and steadily make bigger the duration as you advantage self assurance within the exercise.

Maintain consistency:

Include journaling on your morning routine often, specifically on weekends or whilst traveling. When it involves developing new conduct, consistency is vital, and journaling is not any exception.

Don't worry about being perfect:

Remember that your mag is a consistent region that allows you to precise yourself without worry of judgment or criticism. Don't be involved with being perfect or writing some element insightful every day. Just give attention to the act of writing and the advantages it presents.

Set intentions for the day:

Use your morning journaling workout to set intentions for the day in advance. Write down unique desires or acts you need to take, and do not forget the manner you want to be perceived. This will let you in ultimate centered and brought about for the duration of the day.

Use activates to get began:

If you are having hassle getting started with writing, attempt using activates to get your creative juices flowing. Many journaling activates are available on line or in books to assist encourage your writing.

Chapter 10: Incorporating Self-Care Into Your Morning Routine

Incorporating self-care into your morning ordinary gives severa health, intellectual, and emotional blessings.

Here are most of the benefits to think about:

Reduces strain and anxiety:

Prioritizing yourself-care in the morning can assist restriction anxiety and tension inside the path of the day. Activities which incorporates meditation, yoga, and writing can help you loosen up and experience more focused, foremost to a greater super outlook and stepped forward temper.

Increases productivity:

If you take the time within the morning to care for yourself, you could discover that you are greater green at some degree in the day. You can method your art work with a clearer, more centered attitude if you set out time to attention on what is important.

Boosts creativity:

Doing progressive sports activities activities in the morning, along with writing, sketching, or appearing music, can assist stimulate your mind and enhance creativity at some stage in the day. Starting your day with a innovative outlet can help you to be greater stimulated and effective in special regions of your lifestyles.

Improves bodily health:

Engaging in self-care sports which consist of workout, a healthful eating regimen, and pores and skin care will assist you to enjoy extra energy in a few unspecified time inside the future of the day. Regular exercise enables to increase strength and versatility, even as an top notch weight loss plan can offer your body with the assets it requires to characteristic properly.

Improves relationships:

When you address your self, you may discover that you are extra in a function to connect to others in your existence. Prioritizing your private desires and properly-being allows you to approach your relationships with extra serenity and presence, which could beneficial resource in communique and conventional connection.

Incorporating self-care into your morning ordinary does not need to be time-eating or difficult. Simply devoting a few minutes each day to sports activities that nourish each your body and mind should have a sizeable impact in your standard nicely-being. Whether you meditate, exercising, or devour a nutritious breakfast, prioritizing self-care inside the morning will allow you to start your break day correctly and set the tone for a nice, powerful day.

Tips for incorporating self-care into your morning habitual

Self-care is essential to your physical, intellectual, and emotional nicely-being. Self-care let you begin your day off on a excessive look at and set the tone for the rest of the day. Here are a few pointers for incorporating self-care into your morning routine:

Get up a chunk in advance:

If you want to include self-care for your morning ordinary, you need to offer yourself sufficient time to lighten up. To deliver your self time to recognition on self-care sports activities, attempt waking up 15-half-hour earlier than everyday.

Practice mindfulness:

Mindfulness will allow you to lessen strain and tension while moreover improving your general well-being. Try incorporating mindfulness into your morning ordinary with the aid of way of doing a short meditation, taking some deep breaths, or genuinely taking a few moments to be gift and conscious earlier than starting your day.

Take care of your pores and pores and skin:

Your pores and pores and skin is the most important organ in your frame, and it is important in your modern day fitness. Washing your face, making use of moisturizer, and wearing sunscreen want to all be a part of your morning normal.

Stretch or do yoga:

Stretching or practicing yoga will permit you to awaken your frame at the same time as additionally improving your flexibility and mobility. To get your body transferring and your day started out at the proper foot, attempt along with a few slight stretching or yoga poses for your morning normal.

Eat an exquisite breakfast:

Eating a nutritious breakfast is beneficial in your regular health and will let you sense energized and focused at a few degree within the day. Incorporate healthful meals into your morning ordinary, together with end result, greens, entire grains, and lean protein.

Listen to tune:

Music has a sturdy have an effect on in your temper and feelings. In order to start your day on a immoderate exceptional have a study, try which encompass some uplifting or peaceful tune to your morning ritual.

Make time for something you revel in:

Making time for some thing you revel in will assist you reduce strain and enhance your famous well-being. Incorporate an a laugh hobby or pastime into your morning normal, which includes analyzing, journaling, or working on a puzzle.

Overall, incorporating self-care into your morning recurring is an awesome approach to prioritizing your nicely-being and setting up a top notch tone for the day. By giving your self time to awareness on self-care sports activities activities, you can beautify your temper, lessen stress and anxiety, and experience greater energized and centered in some unspecified time in the future of the day.

Chapter 11: Creating A Family-Friendly Morning Routine

Creating a own family-first-class morning ordinary can be hard, however it is an crucial step to make sure that everybody begins the day without work at the right foot. A well-set up morning routine can assist to reduce pressure and chaos within the morning, promote high-quality conduct and behaviors, and set the extent for a a achievement day in advance.

Here are a few suggestions for growing a morning normal that works for everyone in the own family:

Involve each person inside the making plans machine:

To make certain that the morning habitual works for every body within the family, it is essential to encompass all own family individuals inside the making plans method. Sit down together along with your own family and talk what everybody wants to do within the morning to put together for the day in advance. Encourage anyone to share their thoughts and dreams, and artwork collectively to extend a everyday that accommodates virtually every body's schedules and choices.

Establish a everyday wake-up time:

It's essential to set up a normal wake-up time for anyone in the own family, even on weekends. This lets in to alter all of us's sleep time table and guarantees that everybody has enough time to complete their morning recurring. When really everyone wakes up at the identical time every day, it could moreover assist to set up a feel of shape and recurring, which may be useful for kids.

Create a visible time table:

Creating a visual time desk is an powerful manner to assist younger children apprehend what's anticipated of them and may assist anybody inside the circle of relatives live on path. The agenda need to outline in reality all and sundry's morning regular, together with responsibilities like brushing tooth, getting dressed, and consuming breakfast. You can create a visible schedule the use of pics, stickers, or perhaps a whiteboard.

Prioritize self-care:

Encourage anybody in the family to prioritize self-care sports like workout, meditation, or journaling. This can assist every body start the day with a high quality mind-set and may decorate primary well-being. Consider incorporating self-care sports activities into the morning ordinary, even though it's simplest for a couple of minutes.

Make breakfast a hassle:

Breakfast is an critical meal that could provide the energy and vitamins needed to gasoline the day ahead. Encourage all people within the own family to consume a nutritious breakfast, and recollect making geared up food in advance to preserve time inside the morning. If time is a topic, keep in mind breakfast alternatives which might be quick and easy to put together, like smoothies or overnight oats.

Allow for flexibility:

While it's far important to set up a normal ordinary, it is also important to allow for flexibility even as desired. If a person is feeling ill or desires extra time to complete a assignment, be knowledge and regulate the ordinary as wanted. It's essential to be flexible and adapt the ordinary to meet the changing needs of your family.

Stick to the habitual:

Once you have got installation a morning ordinary, it's crucial to stick to it as an awful lot as feasible. This permits to set up a enjoy of shape and recurring, which can be specifically useful for youngsters. When all of us is privy to what's expected of them in the morning, it can help to reduce stress and chaos and make the morning ordinary smoother and extra a laugh for actually every body..

Chapter 12: Troubleshooting Your Morning Routine

Developing a morning regular is an excellent approach to prepare your self for achievement each day. It will will let you be more efficient, reduce stress, and start your day with a superb attitude. However, even the top notch-laid plans can once in a while cross awry, and your morning recurring is not any exception.

Here are some not unusual problems you may probable come upon collectively together with your morning habitual, as well as some troubleshooting pointers to help you overcome them.

Issue #1: Lack of Motivation

Some days, it can be difficult to find out the inducement to escape from bed, let alone address a morning regular. Whether you are feeling tired, forced, or surely now not inside the mood, a lack of motivation can derail your morning routine in advance than it even gets commenced.

Solution: Identify your Why

When you are feeling unmotivated, it is able to help to remind yourself why your morning regular is crucial to you. Is it to reinforce your productiveness, reduce stress, or prioritize self-care? Whatever your reasons, remind yourself of them each morning to assist kickstart your motivation.

Issue #2: Oversleeping

We all have the ones mornings while we hit the snooze button one too normally and oversleep. But oversleeping can throw off your complete morning everyday, leaving you feeling rushed and confused.

Solution: Adjust Your Bedtime

One manner to prevent oversleeping is to regulate your bedtime. Try to visit mattress a bit in advance every night time time to make sure you have become sufficient sleep, and maintain in mind putting an earlier bedtime on nights earlier than crucial or busy days.

Issue #3: Running Out of Time

Even the most well-deliberate morning workout routines can run into issues whilst there honestly is not sufficient time in the morning. Maybe you hit website traffic in your manner to paintings, in any other case you spent too much time on one task.

Solution: Prioritize Your Tasks

When you are short on time, it's crucial to prioritize the most essential duties to your morning everyday. Consider which obligations are critical and which ones can wait until later within the day. You may additionally moreover want to modify the length of some duties to in form them into your morning ordinary.

Issue #four: Distractions

Distractions can be a number one barrier to a successful morning routine. Whether it is scrolling thru social media or getting out of place in emails, distractions can devour up valuable time and throw off your routine.

Solution: Eliminate Distractions

Try to take away distractions as masses as viable to avoid them. Consider turning off notifications on your cellphone or laptop, and keep away from checking social media or e mail till after your morning normal is complete. You may additionally moreover moreover want to set limitations with family members or roommates to avoid interruptions throughout your morning routine.

Issue #5: Lack of Consistency

In order to gain the blessings of a morning routine, it's miles important to be steady. However, with busy schedules and converting workout routines, it may be difficult to keep consistency for your morning routine.

Solution: Plan for Flexibility

While consistency is critical, it is similarly important to plot for flexibility. This technique spotting that there may be days even as your normal desires to be adjusted or skipped altogether. Rather than beating your self up for missing an afternoon, try and interest on getting decrease again heading within the right path the next day.

Here are some greater recommendations for troubleshooting your morning routine:

SIMPLIFY:

If you discover that your morning recurring is surely too complicated or takes an excessive amount of time, simplify it. Eliminate any useless steps or responsibilities and streamline your everyday.

PRIORITIZE:

If you discover that you are often taking walks out of time in the morning, prioritize your obligations. Determine which duties are most vital and cognizance on finishing the ones first.

ADJUST YOUR SCHEDULE:

If you discover which you are constantly going for walks out of time within the morning, modify your schedule. Try waking up earlier or adjusting the timing of your habitual to offer your self extra time.

STAY CONSISTENT:

Consistency is essential to a successful morning routine. Maintain your normal as masses as viable, even on weekends and vacations.

MAKE ADJUSTMENTS AS NEEDED:

As your existence and time table trade, you can need to make modifications for your morning routine. Stay bendy and willing to make adjustments as needed to preserve your habitual powerful.

DON'T GIVE UP:

It may also make an effort to find the suitable morning ordinary for you. Don't surrender if your ordinary isn't always running in addition to you want at the begin. Keep trying and making modifications till you locate the recurring that works amazing for you.

Chapter 13: Tracking Your Progress And Staying Accountable

Tracking your improvement and staying accountable are critical additives of establishing and retaining a a fulfillment morning normal. By tracking your development, you could see how a protracted way you have got come and make adjustments as desired. And through staying responsible, you can make certain which you are regular to your efforts.

There are many techniques to tune your improvement and live accountable.

One approach is to apply a mag or planner to report your every day sports activities and progress toward your goals.

This can encompass topics just like the time you awaken, the activities you do inside the morning, and any worrying situations or successes you skilled. You also can use this magazine to mirror in your improvement and set new desires for the destiny.

Another way to tune your development is to use era.

There are many apps available that can help you music your behavior, set goals, and show your development. There are a few many well-known examples which lets in you to set reminders, track your development over time, and offer motivation to hold going.

Staying accountable can also be carried out via numerous strategies.

One effective manner is to enlist the help of a chum or member of the family. This man or woman can characteristic an responsibility companion, checking in with you frequently and providing encouragement and guide. You additionally can be a part of a collection or network of humans who've the identical dreams. This can provide a enjoy of community and motivation to keep going.

In addition to those strategies, it's far crucial to have fun your successes along the manner.

This can help to beautify wonderful behavior and provide motivation to preserve. Celebrating successes may be as clean as acknowledging your improvement or treating your self to a few aspect particular.

However you choose out to track your development and stay accountable, it is critical to do not forget that setting up a successful morning normal takes time and effort. It is everyday to revel in problems and stressful conditions alongside the way, but via staying devoted and everyday, you can benefit your dreams and start your time off proper.

Tracking your improvement and staying responsible is an essential a part of any a achievement morning regular. When you music your development, you may see how a long manner you have got come and in that you want to enhance. Staying accountable lets in you live inspired and dedicated in your ordinary.

Here are some guidelines for keeping tune of your improvement and staying accountable:

Set dreams:

Set precise, measurable goals to help you live targeted and advocated. Decide what you want to collect along side your morning ordinary and set goals for this reason. Jot them down and song your development in the direction of them.

Use a dependancy tracker:

A addiction tracker is a smooth device that lets in you music your development closer to your desires. You can use a paper tracker or a virtual one. Simply mark off each day which you entire your morning habitual and spot how constant you're.

Get an obligation partner:

An duty accomplice let you stay at the proper song and provide aid whilst you need it. Choose a person you remember and who's committed to their private morning ordinary.

Check-in on a normal foundation to record development and provide assist.

Celebrate small wins:

Celebrating small wins will let you hold brought on and centered for your dreams. When you acquire a milestone to your morning ordinary, take a 2d to have an amazing time it. Treat your self to a few component small or certainly renowned your development.

Reflect and regulate:

Regularly reflect to your development and regulate your recurring as needed. Take note of what's running nicely and what's no longer, and make changes therefore. This will let you hold prompted and keep away from turning into stagnant.

Chapter 14: The Science Of Habits

In the tapestry of human conduct, behavior is the threads that weave collectively the material of our lives. From the mundane to the tremendous, conduct outline who we are and the way we navigate the location spherical us. In this economic catastrophe, we can delve into the complex worldwide of conduct, records their intellectual underpinnings, and exploring the profound effect they have got on our everyday lives.

The Habit Loop: Cue, Routine, Reward

At the coronary heart of dependancy formation lies the dependancy loop—a neurological machine that governs how conduct are created and sustained. This loop includes 3 key additives: the cue, the recurring, and the reward. Charles Duhigg, creator of "The Power of Habit," brilliantly dissected this loop, dropping light on how we are capable of harness its energy for excellent trade.

The cue is the reason that initiates the dependancy loop. It can be something from a particular time of day to a certain emotional u . S.. Cues create a intellectual and emotional pathway, signaling to our brains that it's time to interact in a particular conduct.

The recurring is the behavior itself, the movement that follows the cue. Whether it's far accomplishing for a sugary snack when feeling pressured or going for a jog even as waking up, exercises are the observable moves that outline our conduct.

The reward is the gratification that comes after completing the regular. It's the mind's way of reinforcing the behavior and growing a preference to copy the dependancy inside the future. Rewards may be physical, emotional, or perhaps mental—a revel in of achievement, a surge of endorphins, or a 2nd of relaxation.

Understanding this loop is pivotal in transforming your conduct. By figuring out the cues that cause your behavior, you advantage the power to redirect the normal and nonetheless experience the same rewards. For instance, if strain triggers the dependancy of engaging in for a sugary snack, you may update the recurring with a short walk or deep breathing physical video games on the same time as nevertheless experiencing the stress consolation you trying to find.

The Neurological Dance of Habit Formation

The thoughts is a complicated orchestra, and addiction formation is one in all its mesmerizing symphonies. At the coronary coronary heart of this method lies the basal ganglia, an area chargeable for procedural reminiscence and the formation of conduct. As you repeat a conduct over time, the basal ganglia takes the reins, freeing up the prefrontal cortex—the choice-making middle—to interest on extra complicated obligations.

This transition from aware decision-making to computerized motion is both a blessing and a capability pitfall. While it lets in us to hold intellectual power, it could also make us vulnerable to terrible habits if we are now not aware. Think about how you results tie your shoelaces or stress the identical path each day. These actions have come to be ingrained behavior, freeing your mind for exceptional obligations.

Rewiring Your Neural Pathways

The plasticity of the thoughts presents a glimmer of preference for the ones looking for to change their behavior. Through intentional effort and repetition, it is possible to rewire the neural pathways that govern behavior. This approach consists of changing antique cues and sporting events with new ones on the identical time as maintaining the rewards.

Neuroscientists have determined that the brain's functionality to form new neural connections, called neuroplasticity, is a lifelong phenomenon. This way that regardless of your age, you've got were given were given the power to form your thoughts's structure. The more you exercise a modern-day addiction, the stronger the associated neural connections end up, grade by grade making the conduct greater automated.

However, rewiring your thoughts requires staying electricity and consistency. The basal ganglia is keen on familiarity, so be organized for resistance as you introduce adjustments. To increase your possibilities of fulfillment, begin with small, attainable adjustments that regularly reason massive shifts in conduct. Remember that behavior are not created in a single day; they are cultivated via committed strive through the years.

The Ripple Effect of Habits

As behavior solidify in our lives, their effect extends a long way beyond the actions themselves. A single addiction can supply ripples throughout various domain names, influencing our emotions, relationships, and ordinary well-being. For instance, continually working towards gratitude can cultivate a wonderful outlook on existence, affecting no longer most effective your thoughts-set however additionally the way you've got got interaction with others.

Furthermore, conduct are interwoven with our identity. The conduct we've got were given interplay in end up a reflection of who we're, shaping our self-perception and how others apprehend us. If you commonly prioritize self-care, it is likely that you may be seen as someone who values their health and nicely-being.

In this financial disaster, we have got scratched the floor of the complicated international of behavior. From the addiction loop to the underlying neurological strategies, we've got were given had been given explored how habits are normal and sustained. As you embark on the adventure of cultivating healthful behavior and sporting activities, recollect that you personal the electricity to form your thoughts, your behavior, and ultimately, your life.

Chapter 15: Identifying Your Goals

In the complicated tapestry of human existence, desires act because the guiding threads that weave our aspirations into truth. They are the compasses that navigate our lives, steering us in the direction of purpose and success. In this chapter, we are capable of embark on a journey of self-discovery, unraveling the significance of setting clean and large desires as the inspiration for cultivating healthful behavior and sports activities.

The Power of Intention

Goals are greater than mere wishes; they'll be intentions sponsored via using a dedication to do so. They provide course and cause, infusing our lives with a revel in of which means and fulfillment. Without clean dreams, our moves end up scattered, our efforts diluted, and our development ambiguous.

Imagine embarking on a adventure without a holiday spot in thoughts. You may additionally wander aimlessly, making picks primarily based on brief goals in place of long-time period aspirations. However, even as you define your vacation spot, each step turns into practical, each choice aligned together with your final imaginative and prescient.

Defining Short-term and Long-time period Objectives

Effective purpose-placing consists of a sensitive balance among brief-term and prolonged-time period targets. Short-term goals are the constructing blocks that purpose large achievements. They provide right now direction and a feel of success as you are making everyday improvement. Long-time period dreams, however, function the guiding stars that mild up your existence's route.

For example, in case your prolonged-term intention is to persuade a more healthy life-style, your quick-time period dreams must embody strolling for 30 minutes each day, decreasing sugar intake, or education mindfulness. These smaller desires not only create a roadmap but moreover provide tangible victories along the way, reinforcing your commitment.

S.M.A.R.T. Goals: The Blueprint for Success

S.M.A.R.T. Goals are a time-tested framework that guarantees your goals are Specific, Measurable, Achievable, Relevant, and Time-tremendous. This technique transforms vague aspirations into actionable goals, improving your opportunities of success.

Specific: Clearly define what you need to gather. The greater precise your aim, the clearer your route will become. Instead of pronouncing, "I want to exercise more," specify, "I will bypass for a 30-minute jog each morning."

Measurable: Establish measurable requirements to music your development. This not simplest keeps you responsible but furthermore gives a sense of fulfillment as you hit milestones. For instance, in case your purpose is to study greater, set a measurable aim like, "I will look at one e-book everyday with month."

Achievable: Your dreams have to venture you without being overwhelming. Consider your present day instances and assets whilst placing goals. Instead of aiming to run a marathon subsequent month and now not the usage of a earlier education, set a motive to complete a 5k run internal six months.

Relevant: Align your goals collectively with your values and prolonged-term aspirations. Ensure that your goals make contributions for your common properly-being and increase. If you fee creativity, a applicable goal may be, "I will spend 30 minutes each day jogging on my paintings responsibilities."

Time-sure: Set a practical time frame for conducting your dreams. A lessen-off date creates a revel in of urgency and prevents procrastination. For instance, in place of pronouncing, "I'll test a present day language sooner or later," set a time-high quality cause like, "I will obtain primary conversational fluency in Spanish indoors 3 hundred and sixty five days."

The Emotional Connection to Goals

While S.M.A.R.T. Dreams provide a established approach, it's far vital to infuse your goals with emotional significance. Emotions are the fuel that propels us ahead while challenges stand up. When you emotionally connect with your desires, they turn out to be greater than checkboxes to tick off; they emerge as property of idea and motivation.

To create an emotional bond collectively collectively with your desires, reflect on why they count number to you. How will challenge those goals impact your life, your relationships, and your conventional nicely-being? Connecting your dreams to your values and passions makes them greater compelling and ignites a fireplace inner you to pursue them relentlessly.

Embracing Flexibility and Adaptability

While setting desires is essential, it's miles in addition essential to approach them with flexibility and flexibility. Life is a dynamic journey, and times can exchange . Your desires should serve as publications, no longer rigid constraints.

When confronted with unexpected disturbing situations or opportunities, be inclined to reevaluate your goals. This does no longer mean giving up; it technique adjusting your route to navigate the changing terrain. Adaptability empowers you to stay aligned with your overarching aspirations at the same time as final open to new possibilities.

In this bankruptcy, we have got delved into the significance of placing smooth and massive desires because the cornerstone of cultivating healthful conduct and sports activities. Goals offer the course, cause, and motivation critical to transform intentions into movements and desires into realities.

Chapter 16: Designing Effective Habits

In the complicated tapestry of everyday life, conduct is the colorful threads that bind our movements together. They are the invisible forces that form our workout routines, our behaviors, and ultimately, our destinies. In this financial ruin, we are able to delve into the artwork of addiction format, exploring the way to create effective conduct that propels us inside the direction of our goals and aspirations.

The Habit Stacking Technique

Imagine conduct as building blocks, every one helping the following to create a strong shape. Habit stacking is a effective approach that leverages this concept through linking new behavior with present ones. This no longer satisfactory streamlines your regular however moreover capitalizes on the herbal glide of your day.

For instance, in case you're looking to encompass a day by day meditation exercising, you can stack it onto your gift addiction of ingesting a morning cup of tea. The act of sipping tea will become the cue in your meditation normal. Over time, this affiliation strengthens, making it much less complex to undertake the new habit.

By anchoring your new dependancy to an gift one, you are harnessing the power of consistency. The familiarity of the installed addiction acts as a motive, growing a continuing transition into your selected behavior.

The Power of Starting Small

The journey of 1000 miles starts offevolved with a unmarried step, and the same principle applies to addiction formation. Starting small is not a sign of insignificance; it's a way rooted in psychology that sets you up for success.

When you intention to introduce a ultra-modern addiction, ruin it down into the smallest feasible motion. For instance, if your cause is to exercise daily, begin with a determination to do virtually one push-up.

The secret is to make the motion so easy which you cannot find an excuse not to do it.

Starting small accomplishes critical subjects. First, it gets rid of the crush that often accompanies drastic adjustments. Second, it establishes a experience of success and consistency, every of that are important for dependancy formation. As your dependancy earnings momentum, you can grade by grade growth the depth or period.

The Gradual Build-Up Approach

Once the inspiration is laid with small actions, it's time to employ the gradual assemble-up method. This includes increasing the complexity or intensity of your dependancy over time. The development is deliberate and methodical, making sure that you do now not burn out or lose motivation.

Continuing with the exercise instance, after reading one push-up, you can add a second one the subsequent week. As you grade by grade growth the load, your body and thoughts alter, making the dependancy extra sustainable. This approach minimizes resistance and complements your opportunities of prolonged-term success.

The Ripple Effect of Keystone Habits

Keystone conduct are the catalysts that set off a sequence response of splendid change in various regions of your lifestyles. These behavior have the electricity to steer a couple of behaviors, growing a domino impact that enhances your normal nicely-being.

For instance, normal exercise can be a keystone addiction. When you make a decision to a workout recurring, you may find out that your consuming behavior enhance, your pressure tiers decrease, and your sleep great complements. By focused on a keystone dependancy, you are strategically triggering a cascade of first rate modifications that boom far beyond the addiction itself.

Identifying and prioritizing keystone habits may additionally have a transformative impact to your lifestyles. As you domesticate those foundational behaviors, you may witness their profound effect rippling thru your sporting activities, relationships, and private increase.

Leveraging Mindfulness in Habit Formation

Mindfulness, the workout of being fully present and aware of the present day 2nd, is a effective tool for dependancy formation. By integrating mindfulness into your behavior, you cultivate a heightened revel in of cognizance that enhances your decision-making and self-interest.

When you have interplay in a dependancy mindfully, you're fully attuned to the sensations, emotions, and mind associated with the behavior. This degree of cognizance allows you discover triggers, cues, and patterns that effect your behavior. As a end result, you switch out to be higher ready to make intentional picks and reshape your wearing occasions.

For example, whilst ingesting mindfully, you pay near interest in your hunger cues, get pleasure from each bite, and recognize when you're whole. This focus can bring about more healthy eating conduct and save you overindulgence.

Celebrating Small Wins and Acknowledging Progress

In the pursuit of dependancy formation, acknowledging your development is paramount. Celebrating small wins reinforces your dedication, boosts your motivation, and creates a wonderful comments loop.

Set up a tool to track your improvement, whether or now not it's far via a magazine, a addiction-monitoring app, or a smooth calendar. Each time you correctly complete your desired conduct, mark it as an fulfillment. Over time, the ones visible cues function a testament in your willpower and encourage you to live the direction.

Remember that the journey of addiction formation is not linear. There can be days whilst motivation wanes, and setbacks arise. During such times, reflecting in your improvement and celebrating your achievements can reignite your enthusiasm and propel you ahead.

In this financial disaster, we've unraveled the art work of dependancy layout, exploring strategies that beautify your functionality to create and hold effective behavior. Habit stacking, beginning small, the gradual construct-up method, and embracing keystone behavior are techniques that lay the basis for lasting change.

By integrating mindfulness and celebrating your improvement, you infuse goal and positivity into your addiction-forming adventure. As you look at those requirements and techniques, you are putting the diploma for the transformative changes as a way to spread within the next chapters.

Chapter 17: Creating A Balanced Routine

In the symphony of life, physical video games are the harmonious melodies that guide us through the cacophony of our days. A well-crafted ordinary offers form, balance, and a sense of rhythm that nurtures our bodily, intellectual, and emotional well-being. In this chapter, we can discover the artwork of making a balanced recurring that enriches each component of your lifestyles.

Embracing the Dance of Daily Routines

A recurring is not a rigid time desk that stifles spontaneity; as an alternative, it is a framework that empowers you to make intentional alternatives. Your ordinary is the canvas upon that you paint the masterpiece of your lifestyles. It's a chain of actions that, at the same time as combined, create a good sized and functional day.

When crafting your habitual, recall the wonderful roles you play—whether as a professional, a companion, a decide, or a pal. Balancing the ones roles calls for thoughtful allocation of time and energy, ensuring that no aspect of your life overshadows the relaxation.

The Morning Ritual: Setting the Tone for the Day

The morning is a clean canvas, ready to be painted with intentions that set the tone for the day beforehand. A well-designed morning ordinary could have an impact in your mind-set, productiveness, and everyday well-being.

Start your morning ritual via using the usage of dedicating time to your self. Whether it's miles meditation, journaling, or mild stretching, interact in sports activities that center your mind and put together you for the demanding situations and opportunities of the day. Nourishing your body with a wholesome breakfast and hydrating your self jumpstarts your physical vitality.

A properly-installed morning regular would now not in fact appear; it requires conscious planning and a self-discipline to prioritize self-care. As you start your day with cause, you are more likely to method the hours that observe with interest, positivity, and resilience.

The Work-Life Harmony

Balancing paintings and personal lifestyles is an ongoing pursuit that desires conscious allocation of time and power. A harmonious everyday acknowledges the importance of every spheres and fosters their integration in area of their separation.

When designing your art work ordinary, set clean obstacles to save you artwork from encroaching for your non-public time. Define precise paintings hours and try and disconnect at the same time because the workday is over. On the opportunity hand, integrate short breaks sooner or later of your work hours to recharge and decorate productiveness.

Incorporate private activities into your ordinary that top off your strength and feed your passions. Whether it is spending remarkable time with cherished ones, pursuing pursuits, or wearing out self-care practices, the ones moments anchor you for your personal lifestyles's essence.

The Mindful Pause: Incorporating Mindfulness Practices

In the hustle and bustle of modern lifestyles, the art of mindfulness gives a respite—a 2nd of pause amidst the chaos. Integrate mindfulness practices into your habitual to domesticate a feel of presence, gratitude, and clarity.

Mindfulness may be woven into different factors of your day. Whether it's far a few minutes of deep respiratory earlier than a assembly, a aware walk in the route of your lunch break, or a gratitude exercising earlier than bedtime, the ones moments of mindfulness decorate your focus and growth your memories.

As you've got were given interaction in mindfulness practices, you're cultivating the skills of being simply present, no matter the scenario. This abilties has a profound impact in your potential to navigate disturbing conditions, make aware options, and get delight from the splendor of every passing second.

The Evening Ritual: A Gateway to Restful Nights

Just due to the fact the morning ritual gadgets the tone for the day, the night ritual prepares the canvas for restful nights and rejuvenation. A nicely-crafted evening recurring acknowledges the importance of winding down and transitioning from the busyness of the day to a peaceful night time time's sleep.

Engage in calming sports activities sports that sign for your body that it's time to unwind. Whether it is studying a ebook, working toward relaxation techniques, or carrying out mild stretching, those moves put together your thoughts and body for relaxation.

Minimize publicity to video show gadgets and stimulating sports within the hour earlier than bedtime. The blue moderate emitted via way of manner of virtual devices can disrupt the producing of melatonin, a hormone that regulates sleep. Instead, create a calming environment that permits your transition into close eye.

Flexibility Within Structure

While carrying occasions provide form and predictability, it is important to keep in thoughts that existence isn't static. Embrace flexibility inner your normal to house unexpected sports activities, converting instances, and the ebb and drift of lifestyles.

A rigid regular can result in frustration at the same time as topics do no longer bypass as planned. By infusing your routine with adaptability, you create a enjoy of freedom and resilience. When surprising opportunities get up or stressful situations emerge, you could make changes with out derailing your complete day.

In this financial catastrophe, we've were given explored the artwork of making a balanced routine that harmonizes the severa dimensions of your life. Your routine is a non-public composition, a melody that resonates together together with your values, aspirations, and nicely-being.

As you layout your normal, recall that it isn't always about perfection; it is about locating a rhythm that aligns collectively collectively with your specific times and goals. A nicely-balanced everyday nurtures your physical electricity, fuels your highbrow readability, and fosters your emotional nicely-being.

By crafting a morning ritual that devices the tone, integrating art work and private life, incorporating mindfulness practices, and growing an night time ritual that embraces relaxation, you're crafting a symphony of conduct that decorate the superb of your lifestyles. With each intentional desire, you are shaping your days right into a tapestry of fulfillment, purpose, and pride.

Chapter 18: Overcoming Challenges And Staying Consistent

In the adventure of cultivating wholesome behavior and sports, traumatic situations are the crossroads in which intentions meet reality. They test our dedication, resilience, and backbone. This financial ruin is a guide to navigate those challenges, improve your motivation, and stay everyday on your route inside the direction of a fulfilling lifestyles.

The Willpower Conundrum

Willpower, the intellectual strength that permits us to face up to temptations and make extremely good picks, is a finite useful beneficial useful resource. Just as a muscle tires with use, our power of will can become depleted over the route of an afternoon. Understanding this idea is essential for designing a habitual that helps prolonged-time period addiction formation.

When you are glowing and energized inside the morning, it is much less hard to make disciplined alternatives. However, because the day progresses and energy of mind diminishes, it becomes difficult to stand as plenty as risky temptations or stick with your recurring. This is why many humans find out themselves making terrible alternatives in the night, even after an afternoon of successful picks.

To overcome the strength of will mission, strategically layout your ordinary to the the front-load your day with critical alternatives. Prioritize your maximum difficult conduct inside the morning while your electricity of thoughts is at its top. As the day unfolds, the ones conduct becomes more computerized, requiring an entire lot plenty less conscious attempt.

The Motivation Roller Coaster

Motivation, like a fickle pal, may be unpredictable. It waxes and wanes, inspired through outside factors, feelings, or maybe the weather. Relying truely on motivation to preserve your behavior is a risky approach, because it's certain to vary.

To counter the incentive curler coaster, cultivate place and determination. Discipline is the bridge that consists of you over the gaps among motivation spikes. When motivation is low, field helps you preserve on along with your regular even at the same time as you do not revel in adore it.

One manner to foster area is to remind your self of your "why." Reconnect with the deeper motives you began your conduct within the first area. These reasons function anchors, pulling you ahead whilst motivation wanes.

Navigating Setbacks with Resilience

Setbacks are an inevitable part of any journey, together with the journey of dependancy formation. They may probably come within the form of unnoticed workout exercises, skipped meditation instructions, or indulging in terrible meals. What subjects most is not the setback itself, however the way you respond to it.

Cultivate resilience thru adopting a boom mind-set. Instead of viewing setbacks as screw ups, see them as opportunities to take a look at and enhance. Reflect on what prompted the setback and how you may prevent it inside the destiny. Treat each setback as a stepping stone towards your final achievement.

Remember, a unmarried setback should now not outline your whole journey. It's a blip on the radar of progress. With determination and the willingness to observe, setbacks can end up effective system for self-discovery and growth.

The Power of Accountability

Accountability is a robust strain that continues us heading inside the right direction, even though our strength of mind falters or motivation wanes. Sharing your dreams and development with a trusted friend, member of the family, or a teach can provide the external manual had to stay consistent.

Consider forming an duty partnership or becoming a member of a group with comparable desires. Sharing your demanding situations, celebrating successes, and receiving encouragement from others can decorate your morale and determination. The knowledge that a person else is invested on your adventure can encourage you to persevere.

Tools for Staying Consistent

Technology offers an array of equipment to useful beneficial useful resource your adventure in the direction of consistency. Habit-tracking apps, calendars, and reminders can characteristic seen cues that deliver a boost on your willpower. Set daily signs for your behavior, and music your improvement to display screen your consistency over the years.

Additionally, gamification can upload an detail of a laugh to dependancy formation. Turning your conduct right into a interest with rewards or demanding conditions can create a revel in of pleasure and engagement. For example, venture yourself to complete a 30-day workout streak or to meditate for a certain amount of consecutive days.

The Dance of Self-Compassion

Amidst the demanding situations and moments of self-doubt, self-compassion is your mild guide. Treat your self with the same kindness and know-how you will offer to a chum coping with comparable struggles. Avoid self-complaint and awful self-speak, that could avoid improvement.

When setbacks get up, reply with self-compassion in preference to self-condemnation. Recognize that setbacks are everyday and part of the boom machine. Use them as opportunities to investigate, adjust, and flow into ahead with renewed strength of will.

In this monetary smash, we've got explored the stressful situations inherent in cultivating healthful behavior and carrying activities, similarly to techniques to triumph over them. The adventure isn't without boundary lines, however it is the manner we navigate the ones stressful conditions that defines our success.

By information the finite nature of power of will, fostering vicinity, and constructing resilience, you are prepared to stand the incentive curler coaster and setbacks with grace and backbone. Embrace obligation, leverage technology, and exercising self-compassion to live steady even within the face of adversity.

Remember, the street to a fulfilling life is not a linear direction. It's a journey entire of twists and turns, peaks and valleys. With every assignment you conquer and setback you overcome, you're shaping your person, deepening your willpower, and inching toward the colorful life you envision.

Chapter 19: Nurturing Physical And Mental Well-Being

In the tapestry of life, our physical and highbrow well-being are the colourful threads that weave collectively the material of our life. The interplay between the ones dimensions is vital for a balanced and best life. In this chapter, we're going to discover the complicated connection amongst bodily and intellectual fitness and the manner cultivating conduct that nurture each can purpose a harmonious and enriched existence.

The Holistic Nature of Well-being

Physical and mental well-being are not remoted domain names; they may be intertwined aspects of a holistic approach to health. A wholesome body allows a healthy thoughts, and a balanced thoughts enhances bodily power. Understanding this interconnectedness is high to designing conduct that sell everyday well-being.

Think of your body as the vessel that contains you through existence's reviews. By nourishing it with right vitamins, workout, and relaxation, you lay the muse for colourful bodily fitness. Similarly, your mind is the compass that guides your mind, feelings, and selections. By working towards mindfulness, dealing with pressure, and cultivating effective intellectual behavior, you beneficial useful resource your intellectual properly-being.

The Synergy of Exercise and Nutrition

Regular exercise and a balanced diet shape the cornerstone of bodily health. The synergy a few of the ones elements need to have profound consequences in your electricity stages, immune feature, and sturdiness.

Engaging in everyday bodily hobby releases endorphins, the "experience-specific" neurotransmitters that uplift your mood and reduce strain. Whether it is strolling, yoga, or dancing, find out a form of exercise that resonates with you and infuse it into your regular.

Equally vital is nutrients—a gas that offers the energy vital for your body's abilities. Strive for a balanced eating regimen wealthy in complete food, fruits, greens, lean proteins, and healthful fats. Mindful ingesting, savoring each chew and taking note of hunger and fullness cues, complements your connection with your body's nutritional wishes.

The Healing Power of Sleep

Sleep is the unsung hero of well-being—a rejuvenating gadget that restores your frame and mind. Prioritizing sleep is crucial for retaining top-rated bodily and highbrow health.

Create a snooze-conducive environment with the resource of manner of keeping your bed room cool, darkish, and quiet. Set a ordinary sleep time desk, aiming for 7-9 hours of excellent sleep each night time time. Avoid virtual gadgets and stimulating sports activities before bedtime, as they are able to intervene with the manufacturing of melatonin, the sleep-regulating hormone.

Quality sleep enhances cognitive feature, emotional resilience, and immune response. As you integrate sleep-enhancing conduct into your recurring, you are making an investment for your widespread energy and putting the extent for powerful and desirable days.

Mindfulness: The Gateway to Mental Well-being

Mental well-being is not surely the absence of mental infection; it's miles a country of thriving, resilience, and emotional balance. The workout of mindfulness is a transformative device for cultivating those characteristics and nurturing your intellectual health.

Mindfulness includes being truly gift in the current 2d, looking at your mind, feelings, and sensations with out judgment. This exercising fosters self-consciousness, emotional regulation, and a enjoy of readability that permeates your each day life.

Incorporate mindfulness into your recurring through practices like meditation, deep respiratory, or conscious walking. These moments of mindfulness provide a sanctuary of calm in the midst of life's needs, allowing you to reply to annoying conditions with equanimity and cultivate a experience of internal peace.

Stress Management: Taming the Modern Beast

In the present day-day worldwide, strain has grow to be a ubiquitous accomplice, affecting each physical and intellectual properly-being. Developing effective pressure manipulate conduct is important for preserving equilibrium within the face of life's wishes.

Engage in stress-comfort sports that resonate with you, whether or now not it's miles analyzing, journaling, taking note of music, or spending time in nature. Prioritize self-care, putting aside moments to recharge and reconnect with your self.

Mindfulness practices, which includes progressive muscle rest or guided imagery, may be effective gadget for managing stress. By watching your pressure triggers and enforcing healthy coping strategies, you are equipping yourself to navigate lifestyles's annoying conditions with grace and resilience.

Emotional Resilience: Cultivating Inner Strength

Emotional resilience is the artwork of bouncing lower back from adversity and maintaining a extraordinary outlook notwithstanding existence's usaand downs. This trait is nurtured via a aggregate of self-recognition, emotional law, and healthful coping mechanisms.

Practice self-compassion via treating yourself with kindness, mainly in a few unspecified time within the future of moments of trouble.

Avoid bad self-talk and embody a increase thoughts-set that perspectives traumatic conditions as opportunities for boom.

Engage in sports activities that nourish your emotional nicely-being, whether or not or not it's miles spending time with loved ones, pursuing pursuits, or carrying out modern expression. By fostering emotional connections and cultivating sports that deliver you pleasure, you're constructing a basis of emotional resilience that allows your mental health.

In this bankruptcy, we have got explored the complicated connection amongst bodily and intellectual nicely-being and the way cultivating behavior that nurture each dimensions can result in a harmonious and enriched life. By spotting the holistic nature of well-being, you have got released right into a journey of self-care and increase that uplifts your frame, mind, and spirit.

Chapter 20: Cultivating Meaningful Relationships

In the complicated mosaic of life, relationships are the colourful solar shades that add depth, splendor, and texture to our critiques. Whether with circle of relatives, pals, colleagues, or romantic companions, our connections with others boom our lifestyles. In this chapter, we are going to discover the significance of considerable relationships, the behavior that nurture them, and the transformative effect they've on our well-being.

The Tapestry of Connection

Human beings are inherently social creatures, confused out for connection and companionship. Meaningful relationships offer a feel of belonging, guide, and shared memories that shade the canvas of our lives. Research continuously suggests that strong social connections are associated with superior highbrow fitness, decreased pressure, or even extended durability.

Consider the relationships to your lifestyles as threads that weave through the fabric of your life. Just as every thread contributes to the overall format, every connection shapes your feelings, thoughts, and everyday well-being. The great of your relationships affects your happiness, resilience, and functionality to navigate lifestyles's stressful conditions.

Nurturing Authentic Connections

In the age of social media and virtual interactions, the artwork of nurturing real connections is extra important than ever. Meaningful relationships are built on receive as actual with, empathy, and proper conversation. Cultivating behavior that prioritize those developments is vital for fostering lasting bonds.

Practice lively listening whilst attractive with others. Show real hobby of their reminiscences, thoughts, and feelings. Empathy—the potential to understand and percent each exclusive person's feelings—is a powerful device for deepening connections.

Put yourself of their shoes and are seeking out to understand their attitude.

Engage in open and sincere conversation. Share your mind, feelings, and critiques authentically. Vulnerability fosters intimacy and lets in others to hook up with your actual self. The workout of energetic and empathetic conversation lays the inspiration for significant relationships that flourish through the years.

Quality Time: The Currency of Connection

Amidst the hustle and bustle of existence, the gift of first-class time is a treasure that strengthens relationships. Allocate time to your normal to spend with cherished ones, unfastened from distractions and time constraints. This have to contain having a heartfelt communication, sharing a meal, or assignment an hobby you each experience.

Quality time is not approximately amount; it's miles about presence and attentiveness. When you invest your undivided hobby, you are speaking your care, recognize, and self-discipline to the connection. These moments of connection create lasting recollections and deepen the bonds that tie you collectively.

Acts of Kindness and Gratitude

Small acts of kindness and expressions of gratitude are like brushstrokes that upload warm temperature and vibrancy for your relationships. These gestures create a pleasant environment, pork up the bond, and nurture a experience of reciprocity.

Incorporate acts of kindness into your everyday, whether or not or not it's far sending an encouraging message, sudden a person with a thoughtful present, or offering assist while wanted. These moves talk your love and appreciation, making the alternative character sense valued and cherished.

Practice gratitude through expressing appreciation for the human beings for your life. Verbalize your thankfulness, write heartfelt notes, or interact in gratitude journaling. The act of recognizing the immoderate incredible features of your relationships enhances your personal nicely-being whilst fostering a lifestyle of positivity and connection.

Conflict Resolution and Compassionate Communication

No relationship is without its demanding conditions and conflicts. However, the way you navigate these moments can outline the direction of your relationships. Cultivating behavior of warfare selection and compassionate communication is vital for maintaining wholesome connections.

Approach conflicts with empathy and a willingness to understand the possibility individual's mind-set. Use "I" statements to express your feelings and needs, keeping off blame or accusations. Create a safe region for open communicate, wherein every parties sense heard and respected.

The exercise of compassionate verbal exchange involves selecting terms which might be thoughtful and kind. Avoid competitive or protecting language, and instead focus on locating commonplace floor and searching out answers. A willpower to resolving conflicts with empathy and appreciate strengthens your relationships and fosters a experience of believe.

Fostering Personal Growth Together

Meaningful relationships aren't stagnant; they're dynamic, evolving entities that might foster non-public increase. By assisting every high-quality's aspirations, hard each precise to be better, and presenting a secure area for vulnerability, you create an surroundings that encourages man or woman and collective transformation.

Encourage open conversations about private desires and desires. Share your aspirations and pay attention to theirs. Collaborate on strategies to useful resource every considered one of a type's increase, whether or no longer it is through responsibility, brainstorming mind, or actually being a sounding board.

Celebrate every one of a kind's successes and milestones. Acknowledge the improvement you have made personally and together. By fostering an surroundings of growth and birthday party, you are nurturing relationships that uplift and inspire each parties to attain their fullest capability.

In this financial wreck, we have got explored the importance of sizable relationships and the conduct that nurture those connections. Just as every thread contributes to the splendor of a tapestry, every dating in your lifestyles contributes to the richness of your research and the extraordinary of your well-being.

Chapter 21: Embracing Lifelong Learning And Growth

In the grand tapestry of human experience, learning and increase are the threads that weave knowledge and depth into the fabric of our lives. The pursuit of data, the cultivation of competencies, and the growth of our horizons form our identification and propel us toward our maximum capacity. In this financial spoil, we can discover the transformative strength of lifelong studying, the conduct that facilitate boom, and the profound impact they have on our personal and professional evolution.

The Ever-Evolving Journey of Learning

Life itself is a perpetual school, offering classes in each enjoy and stumble upon. Lifelong mastering is the commitment to constantly are attempting to find statistics, enlarge perspectives, and growth new talents in some unspecified time in the future of each level of life. This adventure isn't always confined to formal training; it encompasses self-discovery, exploration, and highbrow interest.

Approach each day with the thoughts-set of a scholar, eager to take in insights from severa sources—books, mentors, critiques, and even screw ups. Embrace the way of unlearning previous ideals and adopting sparkling perspectives that align collectively together with your personal boom.

The Role of Curiosity and Humility

Curiosity is the driving strain that fuels the engine of lifelong studying. A curious thoughts seeks solutions, explores possibilities, and ventures into uncharted territories. Cultivating curiosity requires an openness to new mind and a willingness to impeach assumptions.

Approach life with humility, spotting that there's typically extra to investigate. No be counted extensive range how an lousy lot information you collect, there will continuously be big geographical regions geared up to be decided. Humility opens the door to non-forestall boom, allowing you to acquire insights and perspectives from others with gratitude.

Reading: The Gateway to Exploration

Reading is one of the most powerful gadget for obtaining data, growing horizons, and fostering empathy. Whether thru fiction, non-fiction, biographies, or self-assist books, reading gives a window into notable worlds, cultures, and mind.

Incorporate analyzing into your routine, dedicating time every day to have interaction with a whole lot of texts. Whether you are searching out to increase your facts of a particular topic or to escape proper right into a fictional narrative, analyzing nurtures your intellectual and emotional nicely-being.

Skill Development: The Art of Mastery

Skills are the practical manifestations of reading—they're the threads that weave competence and mastery into your life's tapestry. Whether it is learning a musical tool, a brand new language, or a craft, expertise development gives a experience of achievement and reason.

Identify abilities that align collectively along with your hobbies and passions. Break down the mastering manner into potential steps, schooling constantly and deliberately. Set precise desires for talent development, and diploma your progress over the years. Embrace traumatic situations as opportunities to refine your competencies and extend your ability.

Embracing Failure as a Stepping Stone

Failure is not an give up; it is a stepping stone inside the course of boom and development. In the tapestry of lifelong studying, screw ups are the threads that add texture and intensity for your tale. They provide education, resilience, and the humility to well known that fulfillment is often constructed on a foundation of setbacks.

Approach failure with a growth mindset—an know-how that setbacks are short and possibilities for reading. Reflect on what went wrong, find out regions for development, and modify your approach consequently. Every failure is a risk to refine your competencies, refine your strategies, and emerge stronger.

Seeking Mentorship and Collaboration

Mentorship is a powerful catalyst for increase, providing steering, insights, and know-how from the ones who've traversed comparable paths. Engage with mentors who encourage you and might provide valuable recommendation primarily based totally on their reviews.

In addition to mentorship, collaboration with friends and co-workers fosters a dynamic alternate of mind and perspectives. Surround your self with people who undertaking and assist you, growing a community of boom and shared studying.

The Virtue of Adaptability

Lifelong gaining knowledge of is intrinsically tied to adaptability—the capability to encompass trade, evolve, and thrive in new instances. In a global characterised via the use of fast advancements and shifting landscapes, the functionality to conform is crucial for personal and professional success.

Cultivate a mindset of adaptability via the usage of the usage of ultimate open to new mind, technology, and possibilities. Embrace trade as a chance to examine, develop, and growth your talents. This flexibility no longer only keeps you applicable but moreover positions you as a proactive player within the ever-converting tapestry of life.

In this financial ruin, we've explored the transformative strength of lifelong studying and the conduct that facilitate private and expert growth. The adventure of acquiring records, developing competencies, and embracing change provides depth, vibrancy, and which means to the material of your lifestyles.

Through interest, humility, and a dedication to exploration, you're embarking on a journey of non-prevent self-discovery and intellectual growth. Reading, potential improvement, embracing failure, seeking out mentorship, and operating in the course of adaptability are threads that enhance your tapestry with understanding, insight, and resilience.

As you cultivate the behavior of lifelong learning, you are shaping a story of boom, evolution, and boundless capability. Remember that the canvas of your life is expansive, and there are limitless opportunities to weave new threads of facts, talents, and testimonies. With each step you're taking on this journey, you are crafting a masterpiece that shows your curiosity, resilience, and determination to turning into the quality model of yourself.

Chapter 22: Embracing Mindfulness And Finding Inner Peace

In the quick-paced modern global, in which distractions abound and desires are ceaseless, the paintings of mindfulness offers a sanctuary—a secure haven of presence, peace, and self-awareness. Chapter 9 is a profound exploration of mindfulness, its transformative impact on properly-being, and the practices that guide you towards inner peace and readability.

The Essence of Mindfulness

Mindfulness is the workout of being completely present in the 2d, staring at your thoughts, emotions, and sensations without judgment. It's a manner of attractive with life that fosters self-recognition, cultivates gratitude, and complements your connection with the world spherical you.

At its middle, mindfulness is an invitation to shift from autopilot living to aware living. It's approximately acknowledging the beauty in the everyday, the richness in each passing second, and the intensity inner your very personal evaluations.

The Mind-Body Connection

Mindfulness isn't absolutely a intellectual exercising; it is a exercising that bridges the distance among your thoughts and body. The thoughts and body are intricately connected, and the kingdom of 1 affects the kingdom of the opposite. By cultivating mindfulness, you are fostering a harmonious dating among those dimensions.

Mindfulness has been tested to have profound physiological results. It reduces stress hormones, lowers blood strain, and improves immune characteristic. By sporting out mindfulness practices, which incorporates deep breathing or frame scans, you're improving the thoughts-frame connection and nurturing your bodily well-being.

The Power of Presence

In a worldwide complete of distractions and multitasking, the strength of presence is a present. When you've got interplay with obligations and interactions virtually, with out divided interest, you're supplying your undivided presence to the on the spot.

Practice aware presence by way of way of putting off distractions while undertaking sports activities. Whether it's savoring a meal, paying attention to a chum, or taking a walk, immerse your self honestly inside the experience. This exercising enhances your amusement of lifestyles's easy pleasures and deepens your connection with the place.

Mindful Awareness of Thoughts

Our minds are constantly in motion, producing a pass of mind that shape our reports. Mindful reputation of thoughts consists of watching the ones highbrow patterns without judgment or attachment. It's approximately acknowledging thoughts as fleeting phenomena in preference to steady realities.

When negative or stressful mind arise, exercising searching at them with a feel of detachment. This permits you to distance yourself from the thoughts, reducing their energy to persuade your feelings. Mindful cognizance of thoughts empowers you to select which thoughts to interact with and which to allow bypass.

Cultivating Emotional Regulation

Mindfulness is a powerful device for emotional regulation—an functionality to govern and reply to emotions in a balanced and fine manner. By observing emotions as they upward thrust up, you create location a number of the emotion and your response, taking into consideration greater intentional reactions.

In moments of emotional intensity, workout mindfulness with the useful aid of focusing on your breath. This anchors your reputation within the gift 2d and stops reactive responses. Over time, this exercising enhances your emotional resilience and equips you to navigate disturbing situations with grace.

Gratitude and Mindfulness

Gratitude is a herbal companion to mindfulness, as each practices invite you to have interaction with the triumphing moment with appreciation and openness. By cultivating gratitude, you are attuning yourself to the splendor and abundance that exist in each factor of lifestyles.

Practice gratitude via a each day ritual of mirrored photograph. Each day, become aware about three assets you are grateful for. These can be smooth moments, critiques, or connections. This exercise shifts your focus from what is missing to what's sufficient, fostering a feel of contentment and fulfillment.

Mindfulness Meditation

Mindfulness meditation is a proper exercising that hones your potential to be without a doubt gift. It entails dedicating time to take a seat quietly, focusing to your breath, physical sensations, or a particular point of cognizance. As mind rise up, you test them without judgment and lightly return in your element of reputation.

Begin with brief durations and regularly make bigger the period as your exercising deepens. Mindfulness meditation strengthens your mindfulness muscle, enhancing your potential to interact with life's demanding conditions and joys with clarity and calmness.

Cultivating Mindful Living

Mindfulness isn't confined to formal meditation; it's miles a manner of living. Cultivate aware dwelling through integrating mindfulness into your day by day regular. Engage in sports with intention and presence, whether or not it's far washing dishes, taking walks, or interacting with others.

Practice aware respiration sooner or later of the day, taking moments to recognition in your breath and middle your interest. Engage in body scans, in which you systematically study sensations in unique additives of your body. These practices floor you in the present 2nd and cultivate mindfulness on your every day life.

Chapter 9 is an invitation to embark on a journey of mindfulness—an exploration of presence, self-cognizance, and internal peace. By embracing mindfulness, you're unlocking a treasure trove of blessings in your bodily, highbrow, and emotional properly-being.

As you exercise mindfulness, you are cultivating a deeper reference to yourself, improving your capacity to reply to worrying situations with clarity and style, and savoring the richness of every passing 2d. The electricity of mindfulness lies in its simplicity and accessibility, making it a transformative practice that may be woven into each component of your lifestyles's tapestry.

Embrace the practice of mindfulness, and watch because it weaves threads of tranquility, perception, and gratitude into the material of your existence. With every breath, every 2nd of presence, you are nurturing a country of internal calm that radiates at some point of your lifestyles, enriching your evaluations and nurturing your soul.

Chapter 23: Understanding Routine And Happiness

Imagine waking up each day with a feel of motive, readability, and a real smile. The route to the form of lifestyles lies in the marriage of routine and happiness – a connection that holds the capacity to convert our lifestyles into considered taken into consideration one in all contentment, fulfillment, and boundless satisfaction.

Defining Routine and Its Role

Routine, regularly associated with mundane duties and repetitiveness, possesses a hidden treasure trove of possibilities for happiness. At its middle, ordinary is a series of intentional moves and conduct that we consciously integrate into our lives. These conduct offer shape, stability, and rhythm, presenting a revel in of predictability in an ever-converting worldwide. While ordinary may additionally seem proscribing, it surely acts as a canvas upon which we will paint our aspirations, desires, and goals.

In the pursuit of cushty lifestyles, ordinary performs a pivotal function. It offers a reliable framework within which we will domesticate conduct that foster properly-being. Through every day, we harness the electricity of consistency, enabling us to carve out time for sports that nourish our minds, bodies, and spirits. Whether its miles dedicating moments to self-care, sporting out innovative endeavors, or nurturing relationships, habitual gives the fertile ground upon which happiness can flourish.

The Science Behind Happiness and Routine

Have you ever wondered why advantageous workouts leave you feeling invigorated, at the same time as others appear to empty your strength? The answer lies in the complicated dance among habitual and our brain's praise device. Neuroscientific research display that our brains thrive on predictability and styles. When we've got interplay in high top notch workouts, our brain releases revel in-first-rate neurotransmitters like dopamine, developing a experience of pleasure and satisfaction.

Furthermore, routine gives a revel in of success that contributes to our commonplace nicely-being. The finishing touch of duties, even apparently small ones, triggers a release of endorphins, regularly referred to as "happiness hormones." These chemicals infuse us with a feel of success and positivity, encouraging us to maintain pursuing exercises that bring us joy.

However, the genuine magic of ordinary's have an impact on on happiness lies in its ability to reduce desire fatigue. Our brains have a finite capability to make selections within the course of the day. By incorporating high-quality sports into our recurring, we free our minds from the burden of making endless alternatives, thereby retaining highbrow energy for obligations that really rely.

As we navigate via lifestyles's challenges and uncertainties, habitual offers a experience of balance. The predictable nature of ordinary acts as an anchor in the direction of instances of strain, assisting us climate storms and keep a semblance of stability. It's inside the route of those moments that the partnership amongst habitual and happiness shines the brightest, providing a lifeline of comfort and resilience.

In forestall, routine isn't the enemy of spontaneity or adventure; alternatively, it's miles the architect of a comfortable lifestyles. By understanding ordinary's definition and the pivotal function it performs in our properly-being, we pave the manner for a transformative journey. As we dive deeper into the geographical areas of routine and its courting with happiness, we're going to discover the layers of technology, psychology, and private enjoy that make this partnership a powerful catalyst for lasting pleasure.

The Benefits of Establishing a Routine

Life's symphony consists of exercises that convey concord and order to our days. In this bankruptcy, we discover the profound advantages that include embracing workouts due to the fact the threads that weave the material of a snug existence.

Stability and Emotional Well-being

Amidst the ebb and go along with the float of existence's uncertainties, exercises act as a ordinary lighthouse guiding us thru stormy seas. The consolation of a predictable ordinary bestows a experience of balance that is vital for our emotional nicely-being. Knowing what to expect creates a protection net that cushions us from the surprising, decreasing stress and tension. This stability serves as a foundation upon which we will construct our aspirations, nurturing a revel in of protection that emboldens us to explore new horizons. As we domesticate physical activities that align with our values and passions, we infuse every day with purpose and meaning, fostering a deep revel in of contentment.

Enhanced Productivity and Focus

Ever skilled those moments of unheard of reputation and productivity? Routines are the name of the game aspect inside the back of such reports. By incorporating specific duties right proper into a ordinary, we create a highbrow cue that signs our brain to shift right right right into a efficient mode. This phenomenon, referred to as "contextual priming," enhances our overall performance and allows us accomplish responsibilities with extra ease. Routine encourages us to allocate committed time slots for artwork, play, and relaxation, making sure that every 2nd is optimized for optimum output. As we draw close the paintings of handling our time thru physical games, we not only accomplish greater however moreover discover ourselves immersed in a go together with the flow state that fosters satisfaction and a revel in of feat.

Improved Physical Health and Sleep

A nicely-crafted normal has the electricity to sculpt a extra healthy, greater colorful version of ourselves. By dedicating time to physical nicely-being internal our habitual, we infuse our lives with power. Regular exercising, balanced nutrients, and self-care practices come to be non-negotiable additives that make a contribution to our everyday fitness.

Sleep, often underestimated, takes center diploma internal a everyday designed for restorative slumber. Through constant sleep schedules and bedtime rituals, we decorate the excellent of our sleep, permitting our our bodies to recharge and rejuvenate.

Routine additionally acts as a figure of intellectual and emotional fitness. By carving out time for mindfulness, meditation, or other stress-treatment practices, we nurture our minds, growing resilience toward lifestyles's disturbing situations. The sporting activities we set up ripple into our relationships, as emotional properly-being paperwork the cornerstone of healthful interactions with cherished ones.

In this economic smash, we have were given illuminated the tapestry of advantages woven via workouts. Stability and emotional nicely-being, superior productivity and consciousness, and advanced physical fitness and sleep are the treasures that look ahead to folks that embody the paintings of ordinary.

As we maintain our exploration, we will delve deeper into the strategies habitual enriches our lives, demonstrating its ability to raise us to new heights of happiness and contentment.

Chapter 24: Crafting Your Happiness Boosting Routine

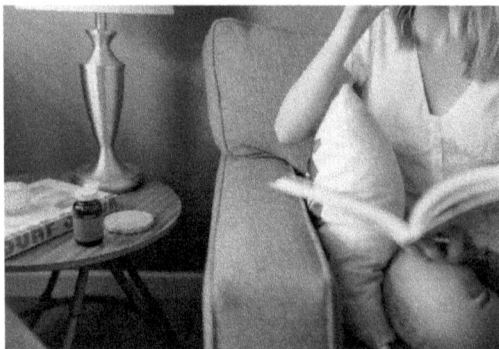

Crafting a recurring is much like growing a masterpiece that shows your specific essence. In this bankruptcy, we delve into the artwork of designing a regular that now not best uplifts your spirit however additionally aligns together with your dreams, values, and individuality.

Identifying Your Goals and Priorities

At the coronary coronary heart of a happiness-boosting everyday lies a deep information of your aspirations and priorities.

Begin by way of the usage of envisioning the lifestyles you preference to influence and the shape of individual you aspire to be. Define your short-term and lengthy-term desires, whether or not they involve personal growth, career achievements, relationships, or properly-being. With the ones goals as your guiding stars, you may find the elements that your ordinary have to encompass.

Consider your values as nicely – the mind that define what subjects most to you. A ordinary constructed on alignment collectively together along with your values has the strength to rouse a profound experience of fulfillment. As you pick out out your desires and priorities, you'll lay the muse for a recurring it is not first-class happiness-centric but additionally motive-pushed.

Tailoring Routine to Your Lifestyle and Personality

Just as each brushstroke contributes to a masterpiece, every component of your ordinary have to resonate together together with your way of life and individual. Acknowledge the limitations and responsibilities of your every day life, and create a routine that suits seamlessly into your cutting-edge commitments. The secret's to strike a balance amongst aspiration and practicality.

Consider your herbal rhythms and possibilities. Are you an early riser who well-knownshows solace in the early hours, or does your creativity flourish in the course of the tranquility of the night time? Align your routine together along with your frame's inner clock to increase its effectiveness. Moreover, understand your non-public strengths and regions for boom. Tailor your ordinary to include sports activities that nurture your strengths even as lightly pushing you in the path of self-improvement.

Remember that a successful normal isn't always approximately perfection however as a substitute about consistency and flexibility. Allow your normal to comply over the years as you have got a take a look at more approximately your self and your desires. By embracing flexibility inside shape, you could create a everyday that is every nurturing and dynamic.

In this bankruptcy, we've got explored the canvas upon which your happiness-boosting recurring will unfold. Identifying your goals and priorities and tailoring your regular on your way of lifestyles and character are essential steps in this progressive technique. As we adventure ahead, we are able to paint the finer information of your habitual, infusing it with practices that domesticate joy, mindfulness, and properly-being, all while last uniquely yours.

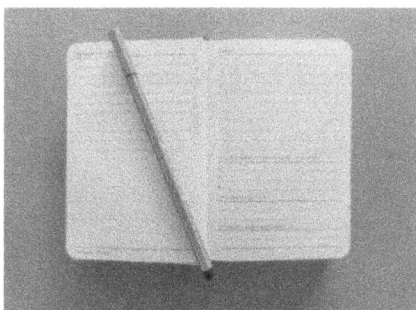

Morning Rituals: Starting Your Day Right

The sunrise of a trendy day presents an opportunity for renewal, and morning rituals are the gateway to a day full of positivity and motive. In this bankruptcy, we delve into the paintings of designing morning workout routines that set the tone for a thrilled and nice day.

Designing an Energizing Morning Routine

Imagine waking as an awful lot as a worldwide of infinite opportunities, a canvas geared up to be painted with moments that invigorate your spirit. An energizing morning ordinary does sincerely that – it jumpstarts your day with enthusiasm and reason. Begin thru infusing your mornings with sports sports that nourish your body and mind.

Chapter 25: Productivity And Time Management Routine

In the canvas of lifestyles, productiveness and time manage are the colours that form our days into masterpieces of feat and boom. This economic disaster delves into the art work of structuring your day for maximum effectiveness and equips you with techniques to live focused and inexperienced.

Structuring Your Day for Maximum Effectiveness

A well-set up day is kind of a symphony in which every phrase contributes to a harmonious melody. Begin through placing easy desires for the day, breaking them down into possible obligations. Prioritize the ones responsibilities primarily based mostly on their importance and urgency, making sure which you cope with the most huge responsibilities at the same time as your strength is at its pinnacle.

Embrace the energy of time blockading, a way in which you allocate unique time slots for precise responsibilities. By dedicating focused intervals to unique sports, you may harness the magic of flow country – a country of deep cognizance and productivity. Integrate breaks into your agenda to recharge your thoughts and prevent burnout.

Create a ordinary that actions a stability amongst artwork and enjoyment. Incorporate sports sports that encourage you, whether or not or now not it's miles a creative pursuit, a stroll in nature, or spending time with loved ones. By nurturing your self outside of hard work, you will infuse your day with pleasure and electricity.

Techniques for Staying Focused and Efficient

Amidst the distractions of the current global, staying targeted is a prized potential. Practice mindfulness inside the path of duties, directing your complete interest to the task at hand. Minimize multitasking, because it dilutes your reputation and reduces the great of your art work.

Utilize strategies at the side of the Pomodoro Technique, which involves operating for a fixed length (e.G., 25 minutes) observed via a quick wreck. This rhythm maximizes awareness and prevents intellectual fatigue. Embrace the Eisenhower Matrix to categorize obligations based totally mostly on their urgency and importance, allowing you to prioritize and manage your workload efficiently.

Digital detoxes, wherein you disconnect from screens periodically, are critical for recharging your thoughts. Create technology-free zones in the course of your day to foster deep art work and creativity.

Chapter 26: Routine For Physical Well-Being

Just as a garden thrives with care and interest, our bodies flourish while nurtured with wholesome behavior. This economic catastrophe delves into the artwork of weaving carrying sports that prioritize bodily nicely-being, focusing on the incorporation of workout, motion, balanced nutrients, and hydration.

Incorporating Exercise and Movement

Exercise is the cornerstone of physical electricity, infusing our our bodies with energy, flexibility, and electricity. Begin via using the use of selecting activities that align together with your alternatives and way of lifestyles. Whether it's miles going for walks, yoga, dancing, or trekking, locate sports activities that bring you delight and lead them to an essential a part of your recurring.

Consistency is top in terms of exercising. Create a schedule that allocates devoted time slots for bodily interest. Incorporate every cardiovascular wearing sports to beautify staying power and power-training sports activities sports to assemble muscle and bone density. Remember, workout is not absolutely approximately achieving aesthetic goals; it is about fostering holistic well-being and enhancing your primary remarkable of lifestyles.

Nurturing Balanced Nutrition and Hydration

The fuel we provide our our our bodies performs a pivotal position in our fitness and energy. Design a everyday that nurtures balanced nutrients through embracing entire, nutrient-rich meals. Plan your meals to consist of some of end result, vegetables, lean proteins, complete grains, and wholesome fat. Be conscious of element sizes to ensure you are nourishing your body with out overindulgence.

Hydration is equally vital. Begin your day with a pitcher of water and hold a reusable water bottle interior reach all through the day.

Adequate hydration facilitates digestion, flow into, and stylish cell characteristic.

Avoid severe diets or deprivation; instead, recognition on cultivating a healthy relationship with meals. Practice aware ingesting, savoring each chunk and being attentive to your frame's hunger and fullness cues.

By incorporating exercise and motion, along with balanced nutrients and hydration, you'll lay the foundation for a wholesome, colourful life. This bankruptcy empowers you to format physical sports that prioritize your bodily well-being, ensuring that you infuse every day with sports and practices that growth your fitness. As we preserve our adventure, we are going to delve into the strategies your everyday can cultivate intellectual and emotional health, developing a harmonious symphony of holistic properly-being.

Nurturing Your Mind: Mental Health and Routine

Just as a lawn desires gentle care to flourish, our minds require nurturing exercises to thrive. This chapter explores the artwork of cultivating intellectual properly-being via practices for pressure cut price, relaxation, cultivating a excessive satisfactory mindset, and going for walks in the direction of self-care.

Practices for Stress Reduction and Relaxation

In a global brimming with wishes and stressful conditions, strain discount and relaxation turn out to be vital equipment for retaining highbrow equilibrium. Incorporate practices inclusive of deep respiration, meditation, and mindfulness into your ordinary. These techniques can help you pause, reconnect with the triumphing 2nd, and create a buffer in opposition to the pressures of every day existence.

Nature has a awesome capability to soothe the mind. Dedicate time to out of doors walks, basking within the beauty of natural surroundings. Engage in sports that carry you joy, whether or now not it is studying, being attentive to tune, or working toward a interest. These moments of rest act as anchors that floor you amidst the currents of strain.

Cultivating Positive Mindset and Self-Care

The seeds of a wonderful mind-set are sown through intentional practices. Begin your day via setting excellent affirmations that form your attitude. Embrace gratitude with the aid of jotting down moments of thankfulness, reminding yourself of the advantages that surround you.

Self-care, regularly not noted, is a cornerstone of highbrow well-being. Design a normal that allows you to prioritize your dreams. This must include placing obstacles, pronouncing no at the same time as vital, and allocating time for sports sports that recharge your spirit. As you invest in self-care, you refill your emotional reserves, permitting you to navigate lifestyles's demanding situations with resilience.

Additionally, include social connections into your everyday. Engage in significant conversations with cherished ones, fostering a useful resource community that bolsters your intellectual fitness.

By nurturing your mind through strain reduction, rest, a extremely good mind-set, and self-care practices, you may create a routine that promotes mental resilience and emotional nicely-being. This monetary disaster empowers you to tend to your intellectual lawn, cultivating a lush landscape of tranquility and positivity. As we improvement, we're going to discover how your normal can further deepen your connections, each within yourself and with those round you, developing a tapestry of holistic nicely-being.

Chapter 27: Winding Down For Peaceful Sleep

As the sun units and the day involves a close to, night time rituals turn out to be the bridge between the bustle of life and the serenity of sleep. This financial disaster delves into the art of crafting nighttime exercise routines that sell rest, prepare your thoughts and body for relaxation, and ensure a non violent night time's sleep.

Crafting a Relaxing Evening Routine

An night time time regular is a sanctuary of calm, inviting you to launch the day's tensions and embody tranquility. Begin with the beneficial useful resource of regularly winding down your sports activities sports because the midnight strategies. Engage in soothing sports activities sports that signal to your thoughts that it's time to transition into rest mode. Dim the lights, play calming tune, or take satisfaction in a heat tub.

Screen time can disrupt your body's natural sleep rhythms. Establish a technology curfew via turning off video display units at the least an hour earlier than bedtime. Engage in sports that sell relaxation, which consist of analyzing a e-book, journaling, or working towards slight stretches.

Strategies for Better Sleep and Rest

Quality sleep is the cornerstone of nicely-being, and your midnight ordinary plays a pivotal role in ensuring restful slumber. Create a everyday sleep agenda by going to bed and waking up at the same time each day. This consistency helps alter your frame's internal clock, optimizing the fine of your sleep.

Create an gold famous sleep environment that allows rest. Ensure your bedroom is darkish, quiet, and without problems cool. Invest in a snug bed and pillows that cater to your sleep choices.

Practicing mindfulness and rest strategies in advance than sleep may be immensely beneficial. Incorporate deep breathing, contemporary muscle rest, or guided imagery into your recurring. These practices assist calm your mind and sign in your body that it's time to unwind.

By crafting an night habitual that promotes relaxation and relaxation, you can make certain that sleep becomes a sanctuary of rejuvenation. This bankruptcy empowers you to layout evenings that honor the transition from interest to relaxation, setting the stage for a peaceful night time time's sleep. As we maintain our exploration, we can delve into the processes your habitual can further enhance your life, fostering a deeper enjoy of connection and achievement.

Building Meaningful Connections: Social and Relationship Routine

Just as stars light up the night time time time sky, our connections with cherished ones moderate up our lives. This financial disaster uncovers the artwork of cultivating giant relationships through wearing sports that prioritize splendid time and improve the bonds that decorate our existence.

Prioritizing Quality Time with Loved Ones

In the whirlwind of present day life, carving out nice time for cherished ones is a testomony to the price we vicinity on the ones relationships. Begin through using identifying the people who be counted number maximum for your life – family, friends, partners – and make intentional efforts to nurture those connections.

Create workouts that facilitate everyday interactions. Whether it's miles own family dinners, weekend outings, or monthly gatherings, those moments come to be threads that weave the cloth of connection. Engage in significant conversations, actively pay interest, and show actual hobby in each unique's lives.

Establishing Routines for Stronger Relationships

Relationships flourish while nurtured through manner of normal. Design rituals that end up shared critiques and loved reminiscences. These should include cooking collectively, embarking on adventures, or taking component in shared pastimes. Consistency on your interactions fosters a experience of safety and bear in mind, developing a robust foundation for deeper connections.

Prioritize open communication inner your relationships. Establish physical sports for checking in, discussing feelings, and addressing problems. A steady vicinity for expression guarantees that misunderstandings are swiftly resolved and emotional bonds are strengthened.

Incorporate acts of kindness and appreciation into your courting habitual. Express gratitude, wonder every unique with considerate gestures, and feature a amazing time achievements collectively. These rituals domesticate an environment of affection and appreciation.

By prioritizing high-quality time and organising exercising exercises that nurture relationships, you'll create a tapestry of connections that enhance your life. This financial disaster empowers you to format routines that commemorate the presence of loved ones, fostering a feel of belonging and joy. As we adventure in advance, we are able to discover how your habitual can further beautify your well-being, aligning alongside aspect your values and passions to create a symphony of contentment and success.

Flexibility within Routine: Embracing Change and Adaptation

Life is a dynamic canvas, painted with ever-changing shades of studies and instances. This financial ruin delves into the art of infusing flexibility into your ordinary, permitting you to gracefully navigate life's transitions, and demanding situations, and balance everyday with spontaneity.

Adapting to Life's Transitions and Challenges

Life is a journey of ebbs and flows, and your routine need to be a depended on accomplice thru its numerous landscapes. Embrace the inevitability of exchange through building adaptability into your normal. Life's transitions, whether they're career shifts, circle of relatives modifications, or personal milestones, require changes on your everyday. Embrace those adjustments with a enjoy of interest and resilience.

Challenges, too, are essential to our boom. Instead of letting them disrupt your normal, combine practices that beneficial aid you for the duration of hard times. Incorporate strain-good deal techniques, mindfulness, and self-care into your recurring, growing a buffer toward life's uncertainties.

Balancing Routine with Spontaneity

While everyday offers shape, spontaneity offers colour and vibrancy for your life. Cultivate the art of balancing the 2 through allowing room for spontaneity inner your regular. Create home home windows of free time that encourage exploration, creativity, and leisure. Spontaneous moments infuse your life with a revel in of aliveness and delight.

Embrace alternate with the aid of viewing it as an possibility for increase instead of a disruption. Approach lifestyles's twists and turns with an open coronary coronary heart and a bendy mind-set. This financial disaster empowers you to weave adaptability and spontaneity into your ordinary, developing a tapestry that evolves with you. As we journey earlier, we will discover the techniques your habitual can deepen your reference to your self and the arena round you, fostering a symphony of harmony and contentment.

Chapter 28: Maintaining Consistency

Consistency is the thread that weaves regular into the fabric of our lives, but demanding situations frequently get up that threaten to get to the lowest of this thread. In this chapter, we find out the artwork of retaining consistency interior your ordinary and overcoming barriers like procrastination, interruptions, and distractions.

Dealing with Procrastination and Interruptions

Procrastination, that foxy thief of time, can undermine your efforts to uphold your routine. Recognize its styles and rent techniques to conquer it. Break obligations into smaller, ability steps, and tackle them one after the other. Set last dates to create a experience of urgency and appoint the "-minute rule," completing responsibilities that can be executed in mins or a extremely good deal plenty less right now.

Interruptions, whether or not or not they come from outside resources or internal distractions, can derail your habitual. Prioritize attention via developing a dedicated workspace, silencing notifications, and putting obstacles with those spherical you. Additionally, communicate your routine to loved ones, garnering their resource and statistics.

Strategies for Staying on Track

Staying heading inside the right route calls for a mixture of discipline and resilience. Employ the energy of addiction thru continuously working closer to your everyday till it turns into 2nd nature. Celebrate your successes, no matter how small, to reinforce your willpower.

Create a visible instance of your regular, whether or not or no longer or now not it's far a tick list, a calendar, or app. Visual cues characteristic reminders and motivation to stick for your routine. Incorporate rewards that align together with your dreams, treating your self for continuously following your regular.

During tough instances, approach your recurring with compassion. Life is a journey, and setbacks are a herbal a part of the method. Reflect in your development and adapt your normal as needed to ensure it stays a sustainable and brilliant strain to your existence.

By getting to know the artwork of consistency and navigating annoying conditions, you may infuse your routine with resilience and resolution. This monetary disaster equips you with the tools to triumph over barriers, making sure that your ordinary stays a steadfast source of well-being and pleasure. As we preserve, we're going to find out how your habitual can generally evolve, developing a masterpiece of contentment and achievement.

Reflection and Growth: Evaluating Your Routine's Impact

As the solar devices on every day, it's time to pause, replicate, and let your ordinary's footprint mild up your route. In this economic catastrophe, we delve into the electricity of introspection, studying a manner to take a look at your recurring's effect and foster non-prevent improvement and private growth.

Tracking Progress and Celebrating Achievements

Every step you are taking alongside your normal's course is a milestone nicely worth acknowledging. Create a region for reflected picture, whether or no longer it's miles a magazine or a virtual record, to report your improvement. Regularly evaluation your journey, noting how your normal has brought on your properly-being, productiveness, relationships, and traditional happiness.

Celebrate your achievements, both huge and small. Recognize the strive you've got invested, and praise your self for reaching milestones. This positivity reinforces your willpower and keeps the fireside of motivation burning.

Continuous Improvement and Personal Growth

Just as plant life acquire for the sun, your recurring want to strive for growth and development. Periodically decide your normal's effectiveness and adjust it to suit your evolving desires and goals. Be open to exchange, embracing new behavior and practices that align in conjunction with your aspirations.

Personal increase walks hand in hand with recurring evaluation. Identify regions in which you've were given thrived and areas wherein you may no matter the reality that blossom. Set new stressful situations and goals, injecting satisfaction and cause into your ordinary.

Remember, growth could now not usually endorse collectively with more; sometimes, it approach refining and simplifying. Streamline your ordinary to consist of activities that genuinely resonate together with your values and priorities.

By assignment mirrored photo and fostering increase, you may make sure that your ordinary remains a dynamic stress to your lifestyles. This financial break empowers you to evaluate the effect of your ordinary and constantly try for non-public evolution. As we adventure forward, we are able to find out the approaches your recurring can deepen your reference to yourself, the location, and the beautiful symphony of satisfaction and contentment that surrounds you.

Sustaining Happiness through Routine: Long-

Term Benefits

Just because of the reality the roots of a tree anchor it firmly in the ground, habitual has the energy to ground your happiness ultimately. In this bankruptcy, we dive into the strategies routine contributes to lasting happiness and explore real-life testimonials and fulfillment testimonies that slight up its transformative capability.

How Routine Contributes to Lasting Happiness

Happiness isn't a fleeting emotion but a nation of being that can be nurtured via steady conduct. Routine gives the framework for cultivating lasting happiness. By weaving high first-class conduct into your ordinary, you create a rhythm of well-being that complements your ordinary exceptional of existence.

Routine gives balance, a revel in of motive, and a supply of contentment. It reduces preference fatigue, freeing your mind to popularity on what honestly topics. As you generally have interaction in sports that deliver you delight, growth your nicely-being, and decorate your connections, you create a reservoir of happiness that sustains you via existence's u.S. Of americaand downs.

Testimonials and Success Stories

Real stories from humans who have embraced recurring as a course to happiness carry its functionality to life. These testimonials display off how regular has empowered people to overcome demanding situations, acquire their desires, and cultivate a sense of fulfillment.

Witness how habitual has transformed morning physical activities into rituals of perception, multiplied productiveness, and heightened mindfulness. Explore stories of humans who've located balance via normal, improving their bodily, mental, and emotional well-being.

These success stories not most effective illustrate the energy of ordinary but additionally encourage you to embark on your personal adventure of sustainable happiness. As you take a look at from the reminiscences of others, you may discover that routine is a precious tool that could lead you to a extra glad and enjoyable life.

By statistics the prolonged-time period benefits of normal and drawing concept from achievement tales, you will help your determination to cultivating lasting happiness. This monetary disaster empowers you to encompass ordinary as a lifeline to nicely-being and contentment. As our exploration continues, we're able to find how your routine can constantly evolve, enriching your existence's tapestry with even greater colorful colorings of achievement and pride.

Chapter 29: Find The Right Time

Finding time for yoga also can appear to be a mission amid the hustle and bustle of ordinary lifestyles, however the proper data is that incorporating yoga into your each day ordinary is more possible than you may count on. In this financial ruin, we are able to discover realistic strategies to discover the proper time to practice yoga, so that you can reap the blessings no matter how busy a while table is.

Identifying the Ideal Moments

The mystery to incorporating yoga into your everyday is to end up aware of the moments that align in conjunction with your strength and availability. If you are a morning individual, thinking about waking up a few minutes early for a revitalizing yoga consultation can be the key. On the opportunity hand, if the night time time is some time of tranquility, putting apart time for yoga in advance than bed can help loosen up your frame and thoughts.

Real Example:

Imagine beginning the day with a sun salutation to rouse your body and thoughts. This can boom your electricity and set a remarkable tone in your sports.

Pro Tip:

Try keeping an electricity diary for each week. Write down the times of the day even as you revel in maximum alert and energetic. This will help you become aware of even as you are most possibly to take time for yoga.

Fitting Yoga into Your Agenda

One of the exceptional topics approximately yoga is its adaptability. You do no longer want an entire hour to acquire the benefits. Even five to 10 minutes of every day practice can make a substantial difference. Look on the breaks on your time desk, such as the lunch smash or the waiting times, and word how you could in shape yoga into those areas.

Real Example:

During your lunch break, you could exercising a few deep breaths and mild stretches. This will now not handiest lighten up your body, but additionally invigorate your thoughts for the afternoon.

Pro Tip:

Set a reminder to your cellphone to remind you to take time for yoga at unique times of the day. This will assist make the workout a natural a part of your normal.

30: Choosing The Appropriate Space

Finding the right region for yoga exercise is simply as vital as locating the proper time. In this financial ruin, we're capable of find out the way to create a tranquil and frightening surroundings to your each day yoga exercise. Remember that your place does no longer need to be extravagant; It need to be a secure haven in which you may hook up with yourself.

Creating Your Yoga Space

If you're schooling at home, pick a place in that you experience snug and non violent. It can be a quiet nook in the bed room, the living room or possibly an outdoor vicinity including the lawn or the balcony. The crucial issue is that you can loosen up and awareness on your exercise with out distractions.

Real Example:

Turn an empty corner on your bed room right into a cushty yoga vicinity. Place a yoga mat, some cushions and a plant to create a serene atmosphere.

Stay organized

Keeping your yoga region organized is important for a a hit exercising. Make advantageous the place is clean and free of muddle. Not great does this create a enjoy of calm, however it also enables lessen distractions even as you reputation on postures and respiration.

Real Example:

Remove any non-yoga related objects from vicinity. Keep only the rug, cushions, and any accessories you use inside the route of workout.

Create a Relaxing Atmosphere

Use factors that promote rest and quietness. Soft lighting, aromatherapy, and soothing song can help set the right mood on your exercising. If you want incense or scented candles, this will moreover make contributions to a pleasing sensory enjoy.

Real Example:

Light an aromatic candle in advance than you begin your practice. The mild aroma can assist lighten up your mind and put together you for the workout of yoga.

Pro Tip:

Try growing a relaxing track playlist for your yoga exercising. Soft, melodic tune can create a non violent surroundings during exercise.

Adapting to Limited Spaces

If you're working towards in a small area, do not worry. Yoga is enormously adaptable and may be finished in any to be had region. If you do now not have masses room for a yoga mat, use a thinner mat or maybe a towel.

Real Example:

If you are at paintings, use a vacant location inside the break room or even an empty meeting room for short and discreet practice.

Remember that irrespective of the dimensions of the gap, the maximum crucial element is to create an environment wherein you enjoy snug and snug to hook up with your self. In the subsequent chapter, we are going to find out brief, powerful yoga practices that you can without issue incorporate into your each day normal.

www.ingramcontent.com/pod-product-compliance
Lightning Source LLC
Chambersburg PA
CBHW051728020426
42333CB00014B/1202